THE BOOK OF JOB
AS A GREEK TRAGEDY

ADVISORY EDITOR TO DRAMABOOKS: ERIC BENTLEY

THE BOOK OF JOB
AS A GREEK TRAGEDY

with AN ESSAY

BY

HORACE M. KALLEN

INTRODUCTION

BY THE LATE

PROFESSOR GEORGE FOOTE MOORE

Bible. O.T. Job. English. 1959.

A DRAMABOOK

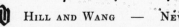
HILL AND WANG — NEW YORK

Copyright 1918 by Moffat, Yard and Company
© 1959 by Horace Meyer Kallen

Library of Congress Catalog Card Number: 59-12602

Manufactured in the United States of America

PREFACE, 1959

It is now more than half a century since I restored the Book of Job of the Old Testament to what I believe was its original form—that of a Greek tragedy in the manner of Euripides.

During this interval the restoration has been occasionally produced by college societies, and given public readings by liberal religious groups; in 1926 it had several professional performances: Sam Jaffe played Job; Wladimir Nelidoff, sometime director of the Imperial Dramatic Theatre of Moscow, was in charge of the production, giving it the correct Greek staging, which the directions added to the restored text did not, for practical reasons, provide for.

In the course of this same interval many alternative renderings of the biblical text have been published, many the work of specialists, others of men of letters caught up by "the problem of Job." None, so far as I know, have given their renderings any kind of dramatic form; [1] nor have any of the critical interpretations of the tragedy, its origins, its meanings, its purpose, and its relation to the historic experiences and beliefs of the Jewish people, brought the Hellenic influence into the

---

[1] A recent analysis of the structure of Job by Claus Westermann (*Der Aufbau des Buches Hiob*, 1956, Tubingen) finds it to be neither a debate nor a dialogue, but an action between Job, his comforters, and God, thus "in reality a drama."

vii

ecology of Job. There is a consensus that the text
draws upon an earlier prose story, a folk tale, of which
Job's author has kept the beginning and the end. Concerning the date of the work, opinions vary. Some of
the learned put it as far back as the sixth century B.C.;
others as late as the third century; still others assign
it to the fifth or fourth. One opinion all can share is
that the prose of the Prologue and Epilogue may rightly
be dated sometime after the Persian conquest of Babylonia, and before the composition of Ecclesiasticus, 190
B.C. The rest is an open field of imaginative reconstruction by theologians, philologists, historians, philosophers, poets, playwrights, and professors of apologetics.
Such reconstructions, however learned and skillful, are
willy-nilly projections of their authors' faith and fan-
tasies. However he makes them, the scholar or critic,
even as the poet, uses what he guesses or believes he
knows to support a hunch or confirm a speculation,
hunch and speculation serving him as working hypotheses. Very often the hypotheses turn out to be the
interpreter's prejudices hardened into inexorable principles. But so long as he stays within the conventions of
his guild this need not afflict him; he may dogmatize and
dispute and even seem to inquire, freely and safely.
Should he, however, disregard the conventions from
within or without, his temerity may make him an
Ishmael, or even a Job.

In the nature of things all reconstructions of the past
are ineluctably bets on uncertainties, postulations on an
as if, rationalizations and more or less calculated risks.
Concerning reconstructions of the Book of Job, I have
not yet found in any a sufficient reason for altering my

judgment, first: that it is the work of a Hebrew poet aware of Euripides' tragic form but un-Greek in his emulation of it; second, that he followed the Greek precedent by framing his heresy in orthodox events and symbols; third, that the form he gave his tragedy was scrambled from the dramatic to the narrative when Job was added to the canonical Scriptures; it was addled in order to fit it into the conventional perspectives of the dominant Judaism of the time. As editors and revisers, the keepers of these perspectives were, when compared with their reconstructioning epigons of the nineteenth and twentieth centuries, simple, clumsy, naive believers, purposing obvious conformations and not detailed re-composition. As the Book of Job looks in the canon, their desire was both to make it a part of Scripture and to vindicate their own faith with it.

Of their faith, the folk tale from which the author of Job draws his tragedy is a self-evident expression. Its beginning and end, which the poet retained as Prologue and Epilogue, by themselves vindicate the orthodoxy that Job's comforters in the play—Eliphaz, Bildad, and Zophar—diversely press upon their unyielding tortured friend. The authorities responsible for including Job in the biblical canon may have felt that they had accomplished what was necessary when they had reshaped the poetic drama to the form of the prose tale. In their reading, Job could not but have lost his case. In the author's writing, however, orthodox Prologue and Epilogue may well have figured as the protective visor for his utter heresy, which he so boldly has Yahweh himself vindicate, twice saying to Eliphaz and his companions in orthodoxy: *My wrath is kindled against thee and thy*

*two friends, for ye have not spoken of me the thing that
is right, as my servant Job hath.*

These words of the Lord occur both times in the first
paragraphs of the Epilogue (chapter 42, 7–10 of the
Bible Job). The paragraphs obviously do belong with
the Tragedy and do not belong with the conventionally
happy ending of the prose tale which serves as Epilogue.
They count rather for an ironic transition to that conclusion of the original story. Their parallel in the Prologue are the lines (Scriptural Job chapter 2, 11–13)
the poet added in order to introduce Eliphaz and his
companions: there is no evidence that they figured at all
in the folk tale.

In what is called "the Great Tradition" the image of
Job is the character in the Tragedy's Prologue and
Epilogue. The Job of the Prologue is a character all
patience and piety who accepts the undeserved afflictions
his anthropomorphic God sends him as he had accepted
his largesse: *Naked came I forth from my mother's
womb, and naked shall I return: Yahweh gave and
Yahweh has taken away; blessed be the name of Yahweh.*
The Epilogue presents Job with his flesh renewed, his
fortunes restored, his patience and piety rewarded with
"twice as much as he had before." Poets and playwrights of the Great Tradition conspicuously draw their
inspiration from the Prologue of the Tragedy.[1]

[1] In sixteenth century England, after the Bible had been joined
to the Greek and Latin classics as a subject of humanistic as well
as religious study, schoolmasters used on occasion to take Job for
the theme of the plays they would write in Latin for their boys to
act. The record takes specific note of Ralph Radcliff's Latin *Job,*
lost like all others of the species.

For example, Goethe opens his *Faust* with a "Prologue in Heaven" and transvalues Yahweh's directive to the Adversary into Mephistopheles' offer to bet the Lord that he can win Faust's soul by satisfying his "desires and aspirations." Indeed, Faust is a sort of Job in reverse; where Job is tempted through his losses and sufferings, Faust is tempted through his acquisitions and gratifications until he shall gorge even dust with zest: *Staub soll er fressen, und mit Lust.* MacLeish's *J.B.* draws almost entirely upon the Prologue, presenting Job's losses and sufferings in modern symbols and the modern manner; either because of unsublimated Christian sentiment, or because he is aware of the apocryphal *Testament of Job*,[1] he makes of Job's wife—whom the Prologue of the biblical Tragedy briefly presents in such a role that St. Augustine condemns her as the Devil's helper, and who then appears no more—a central character in *J.B.*, compensating disaster by love. Josiah Royce has left us, in *The Problem of Job*, a representative repristination of this perspective from the standpoint of America's most freely devout spokesman for transcendental idealism. Recently Carl Jung felt it needful to make his own "reply to Job." This *Antwort auf Hiob* imagines the canonical Job to mark the beginning of the humanization of the cruel, ruthless, immoral Jehovah of the Old Testament into the agapastic God of Love of the New Testament, and this humanization consummated by the Roman Catholic dogma that the loving Virgin Mother of God has been assumed to heaven in the flesh. Even the late Bertold

---

[1] In the *Testament*, Job's wife stays by her husband and sells her hair in order to support him.

Brecht's highly cryptic allegorical morality *Badener Lehrstück vom Einverstandniss* is declared to be somehow a mutation upon the biblical Job, although why, except for the report that Brecht once told somebody that his favorite book was the Bible, I have not been able to make out.[1] If this be in fact the case, Brecht too had a greater care for the Prologue and Epilogue than the Tragedy.

Such a concern is natural enough. It is a matrix of orthodoxy. Whatever be the beginning and the middle of a play or a tale, commonly we crave, we argue, we insist that its end shall be happy, let its form be as God wills. This inveterate and ever-unsatisfied hunger of the heart, which impelled the canonical masking of the Tragedy of Job by the form the Bible preserves it in, has motivated the bulk of its traditional reinterpretations. Works of art, whether graphic, philosophical, or dramatic, have rarely accepted the tragic intention of the Tragedy of Job. This is the warfare, both hot and cold, waged by passionate vindicators of the moral goodness of omnipotent divinity against seers and thinkers who charge this omnipotence with heedless amorality or malice; it is the victory in defeat of those seers and thinkers. This is what so moved the painter-poet, William Blake, that his engravings of the Book of Job stand as the most graphically expressive and symbolically creative of all his masterworks. This is what so impressed Percy Shelley that he at one time planned a classical rendering of the Book of Job. He felt Job to be a blood brother of Prometheus: a daemonic

[1] In an unpublished essay by Lee Baxandall, who has made a translation of the *Lehrstück*.

hero facing up to the overwhelming power of an arbitrary tyrant. And when he decided on Prometheus
rather than Job for his theme, he discarded Aeschylus'
reconciliation of Prometheus with Zeus, for one closer
to the Joban conclusion: neither reconciliation nor submission, but recognition. "The moral interest of the
fable," Shelley wrote, "would be annihilated if we could
conceive him [Prometheus] unsaying his high language
and quailing before his successful and perfidious adversary."

In somewhat like manner, George Santayana gives
the Joban intention new birth in his "theological
tragedy," *Lucifer*, designed to disclose, by the action
of symbolic figures drawn from the Christian and classical legends, the unyielding independence of disillu-
sioned Reason confronting the false moral pretensions
of God omnipotent. Reason is Lucifer. His Tragedy
consummates with him lonely and alone upon his barren
rock, calling upon truth, "eternal bitter truth" to be
his refuge when all else is blind; accepting the not-
unkindness of truth's "joyless bosom," as Job at last
accepted the self-disclosure of Yahweh.

> Lo! I lift my head
> Into the void, in scorn of all that live
> Through hope and anguish and insensate wars.
> For knowing grief, I have forgot to grieve,
> And having suffered, without tears receive
> The visitations of my kindred stars.

This ultimate loneliness is what Job's tragedy con-
veys to Thomas Wolfe: "the most tragic, sublime and
beautiful expression of loneliness which I have ever read

is the Book of Job." Wolfe tells this in a lyrical essay entitled *The Anatomy of Loneliness*, a prose dithyramb on the meaning of loneliness in his experience. "The essence of human tragedy," he writes further, "is in loneliness, not in conflict". . . and adds, "just as the great tragic writer [of tragedies]—Job, Sophocles, Dante, Milton, Swift, Dostoevski—has always been a lonely man, so has he also been a man who loved life best and had the deepest sense of joy." The conventional conception of Job as the patient, silent sufferer belies him. Rather does Job "wear at the heart of its tremendous chant of everlasting sorrow the exalting song of everlasting joy . . . joy solemn and triumphant, stern, lonely everlasting joy which has in it the full depth and humility of man's wonder, his sense of glory and his feeling of awe before the mystery of the universe." Job is the dramatic high place of the sense of loneliness which all the Old Testament utters, even as the words of Christ are the vital center of the New Testament, words whose "total import was that the life of loneliness could be destroyed by the life of love."

Wolfe cannot consent to this consequence. Nor can any of the other lonely men—"the nameless, voiceless, faceless atoms of this earth as well as Job and Everyman and Swift." Nor, in truth, could Christ, that preacher of "the life of love" who was "as lonely as any man that ever lived" and who "died in loneliness."

Thomas Wolfe's assimilation of Christ to Job and therein his aversion from love to loneliness, when set beside the utterances of Carl Jung and Archibald MacLeish, reincarnates the perennial challenge of Job to his comforters and their God. It might seem a strange alliance, but we could rank Robert Frost beside Wolfe. Upon Frost, too, there seems to have lain an inward compulsion to meditate upon Job, to reincarnate and reappraise its tragedy for his own place and time. Frost calls this avatar "A Masque of Reason." Its theme is also the theme of the poet of Job: the tragedy's vital heresy, not the orthodoxy of Prologue and Epilogue. Its concluding line is the italicized parenthesis: (*Here endeth chapter forty-three of Job*). The kindly laughter of the ironical, compassionate humanist who is the Nestor of poetry in America twenty centuries after Christ, replaces with Job's wife the comforters whom the ironic Hebrew poet of the fourth century before Christ had given Job. Frost's "Masque" is a confrontation of God, Job, Job's wife, and the Devil, a confrontation which reappraises, without agony, the imperishable issue between Man and God and Devil.

God begins by gratefully acknowledging what Job had done for him.

> I had to prosper good and punish evil.
> You changed all that. You set me free to reign.
> You are the Emancipator of your God
> And as such I promote you to a saint.

But Job can't stop questioning. *Why I? Why at my expense? What the divine design? What the reason?* until at last God answers:

I was just showing off to the Devil, Job
As is set forth in Chapters One and Two. . . . Do you
   mind?
. . . Your comforters were wrong"

He calls up the Devil, so unreal and ghostly to the modern mind, but in the eyes of Job's wife, "God's best inspiration." The "Masque" ends with her taking a picture of Job, God, and Devil, admonishing them:

> Now if you three have settled anything
> You'd as well smile as frown on the occasion.

Her admonition I take to be the mystical disclosure of why Robert Frost called his masque a Masque of Reason, and why his humanism rings truer than any other epigonic version to the spirit of the Hebrew Tragedy of Job. It helps, as the forty-third American chapter which its poet adds to the forty-two Hebrew ones, to establish why, of all books in the biblical canon, the poetic drama of Hebrew Job concurs best with whatever is modern and not merely contemporary in the faith of modern man.

HORACE M. KALLEN.

New York
5 May 1959

PREFACE TO FIRST EDITION

The accidents of opinion exhibit an ironic and peculiar indifference toward what historians or scientists call " the truth." The forces of nature, the qualities of men, the works of the spirit we call art, have influenced civilization hardly at all by what they were in fact, but deeply and overwhelmingly by what mankind in fancy opined them to be. Fundamental as are tangible realities to the life of man, they remain at best only anchors and stabilizers for ideas. Thinking, some philosopher has said, is thinging. The history of civilization is mainly a history of ideas — their rise, their ripening, their clash, their community; and what science calls today " false " has figured among them far more largely than what science calls today " true."

The present work is the record and result of reflections to which I was compelled by an enduring curiosity about the origin, character, and significance of the false, but very powerful and very ironic tradition concerning the life and labor of the children of Israel. This curiosity has driven me into many fields where I am the merest amateur and worse, and into others where the most expert is equally with the uninitiate a Childe Roland at the Dark Tower. Such guidance as was possible for me I owe to the kindness and tolerant sympathy of Professor George Foot Moore, whose great-minded scholarship treats even tyros as if they mattered, and to the patient expositions of my father, the late

Rabbi Jacob David Kallen, whose narrative of the traditional Jewish commentaries on Job has helped me to choose between alternative readings of the text. Such testing of the results of my imaginative adventure into literary history as the actual production of the restored Tragedy of Job could achieve, I owe to the artistic courage of Mr. T. H. Dickinson and the fine devotion to Hebraic culture of the Harvard Menorah Society. In 1913 Mr. Dickinson, then leader of the Wisconsin Dramatic Society, gave two performances of the Tragedy, one in Milwaukee and one in Madison; and in 1916, the Harvard Menorah Society, celebrating its tenth anniversary, gave a performance of the Tragedy in Boston. Perhaps the courtesy of Professor Moore and the conscientiousness of the producers have caused me more than warranted confidence. I feel, at the present writing, that what I have set down in this volume is sublimation of such conjecture concerning The Book of Job as historic method permits. But contrariwise, it may be — romance. Should the reader come to think it romance, he will also, I trust, recall, that it is not without a goodly fellowship, compact of thousands of volumes of far, far solider learning, yet no less than this slight thing the winnings of merely adventuring speculation about historic and literary origins, relationships, and meanings. The scholar's world, like the story-teller's, is the world of ideas, indeed, and it is true that most of them are false ideas. Were most not false, there would be no generations of scholars to count.

Madison,   HORACE M. KALLEN.
15 October, 1917.

CONTENTS

INTRODUCTION

In 1587 Theodore Beza began a course of lectures on Job in Geneva by dividing the book into acts and scenes, and in the following period several similar attempts were made. Lowth tells us in the 18th century that scholars all but universally regarded Job as a drama; they counted the acts, and discussed the structure of the play, the catastrophe, the introduction of the *deus ex machina*, just as if they were handling an Attic tragedy. In his volume on Hebrew Poetry (1753), which in so many ways makes an era in the subject, Lowth devotes an entire lecture to this question. Taking Aristotle's Poetics as an incontestible criterion, he finds that, although Job has all the other marks of tragedy, it lacks precisely the essential element, the " *actio*." This does not mean — it may not be quite superfluous to remark — that it is not suitable for *acting;* tragedies intended to be read, not played, were written before Aristotle's time, and he himself observes that the proper power of tragedy is felt without scenery, costume, or actors. The " action " which Aristotle demands and Lowth misses is something doing in the drama itself, the doing in which the story, " the soul of the drama," is unfolded, and by which the tragic event is determined and brought about. Lowth concludes that Job may be called a dramatic poem, but not properly a drama. This has become a critical common place; but the criterion has been forgotten, and modern scholars sometimes repeat Lowth's argument, which proves at most that Job does not correspond to Aristotle's philosophy of the drama — not character nor sentiments, but only *deeds* are the cause of men's weal or woe — as a demonstration that Job can not in any sense properly be called a drama. From this orthodoxy there have been some eminent dissidents; Ewald, for example, held that Job is a true drama, constructed with conspicuous art on the necessary principles which are fundamental not merely to Greek tragedy but to all tragedy, and lacking only a formal adaptation to the stage. Dr. Kallen goes a long way beyond these predecessors, however, in his theory that Job is, so to say, a Greek tragedy in Hebrew, specifically modelled after Euripides.

Yet, as if to illustrate anew the trite observation that there is nothing quite new under the sun, the opinion that Job is an imitation of a Greek tragedy was enounced by Theodore of Mopsuestia (d. 428), the most critical head among the teachers of the ancient church. The author of the book, according to Theodore, being familiar with Greek literature and a friend of the Greeks (i. e., the pagans), prompted by an unholy literary ambition, made out of the ancient true story of the Edomite Job a drama after the pattern of the Greek poets, inventing the speeches he put in the mouths of the characters — some of which are injurious and almost blasphemous — as well as the prologue in heaven with its scandalous wager between God and Satan, and the mythical monsters in chapters 40–41. Theodore consequently excluded Job from his Bible as a work of fiction. This, among other errors, was condemned

at Constantinople in 553, and with them is embalmed
in the acts of the Council.

I must not here anticipate Dr. Kallen's exposition of
his hypothesis. The most striking feature of his reconstruction is that it provides a reason for being and
a suitable place for parts of the book which recent
critics have commonly set aside as additions or interpolations, on the ground that they interrupt or suspend
the movement of the poem, or are incongruous with the
tenor of the whole or the person of the speaker, or seem
to be mere purple patches. Such are the praise of
wisdom in chapter 28, the pictures of the way of the
oppressor and the fate of the oppressed classes in 24,
and the description of Behemoth and Leviathan in 40,
15–41, 26. These passages are assigned by Dr. Kallen to the chorus, and so transposed that each round
of the great debate is followed by a choral ode, chapter
28 being introduced after 14, in the place of the first
stasimon; chapter 24, 2–24 after 21; and 40, 15–41,
26 after 31. The relation of these choruses to the pre-
ceding dialogue is no looser than is often the case in
later Greek tragedies; and the differences between them
and the speeches in diction and poetical form, which
have been with the critics additional reason for attrib-
uting them to different authors, are only what would
be expected in choral parts. Elihu is the coryphæus
— which accounts for his not being named among the
dramatis personae (2, 11) — and room is thus made
in the organization of the poem for his speeches
(chaps. 32–37); this suspension of the appearance of
God in response to Job's challenge (31, 35) is drama-
tically effective. The voice of the invisible God out of
the whirlwind is the Jewish counterpart of the *deus ex*

machina, frequently resorted to by Euripides with diverse intent and effect. Finally, the prologue and epilogue fall into place as integral parts of the drama after the Euripidean pattern.

It will be seen that this ingenious hypothesis is in a critical sense very conservative. It does not assume that the book has come into our hands exactly as it left the author's; Dr. Kallen thinks that the choral odes were shifted from their place and concealed in the dialogue to disguise the resemblance to a Greek play, and that there have been minor additions and alterations, but he finds no extensive excisions necessary.

With several recent critics, Dr. Kallen dates the composition of Job about 400 before our era, and he suggests various ways in which the author might at that time have got such acquaintance as he has with the Greek drama. For that matter, the range of possibilities is as wide as the wanderings of the Jews; it is in no wise beyond imagination that he should have seen a tragedy of Euripides exhibited at Athens itself; or at Naucratis, an ancient Greek commercial city on the Canopic branch of the Nile, a conjecture which his interest in the wonders of Egypt might be thought to commend.

The question will be asked whether, in the light of what we know of the chronology of Hebrew literature and the history of the Hebrew language, it is possible that such a poem as Job can be the product of so late a century. A generation ago most scholars would probably have replied with a more or less emphatic negative. Today the " veto of philology " is hardly to be feared. Closer study of the literature of the Persian and Greek periods has shown that many confident

opinions formerly entertained about the decadence of
the language were erroneous. The influence of the
Aramaic vernacular appears in the vocabulary, as it
does to some extent in Job, but Hebrew of unimpeach-
able structure and of notable power and beauty was
written through all this time, and that not as a " dead
language " but as a living literary tradition. It has
been surmised by more than one recent commentator
that the employment of dialogue in Job for the discus-
sion of high themes is in some way dependent on the
writings of Plato, a generation later than Euripides;
and considerable parts of Job, including not only the
speeches of Elihu but the splendid eulogy of wisdom in
chapter 28, have of late frequently been ascribed to the
third century, which shows at least that competent
scholars find no philological difficulty in such a date.

Wherever the form of the Book of Job may have come
from, and notwithstanding the fact that the author by
his choice of scene and characters clearly indicates that
he would have his problem conceived as a universal
human problem, excluding all that is nationally Jewish
even in religion, the matter is Jewish; and this Dr.
Kallen discusses in a second introductory essay on
" The Joban Philosophy of Life," an interpretation of
the problem of the book and its solution — for, contrary to many recent commentators, he finds a solution
in it. The outcome, as he apprehends it, is an idea of
God and a theory of life in which the process of the
Hebrew religion, first moralizing and then deperson-
alizing God, culminates, and in which the " ripest wisdom of the Hebraic mind finds expression." An in-
teresting comparison might be made with a chapter of
Marcus Aurelius (ix, 1) on the neutrality of the Uni-

versal Nature and the attitude of the man who knows his place in nature.

It would be a mistake to regard " The Book of Job as a Greek Tragedy " as an ingenious paradox; it is a serious hypothesis which invites serious consideration from Biblical scholars and students of literature.

GEORGE F. MOORE.

Cambridge,
    February 11, 1918.

THE ORIGINAL FORM AND PHILOSOPHIC
MEANING OF THE BOOK OF JOB

THE BOOK OF JOB AS A GREEK TRAGEDY

I

§ 1. *Greek Influence on Hebrew Life and Letters.*

Was the Book of Job written as a Greek tragedy?
Yes. The following considerations show why. Although the Jews of to-day bear to the drama a relation considered by many to be more intimate than agreeable, neither their immediate nor their remote ancestors showed much concern for this form of art. Indeed, to the Jews of our own age writing for the stage or acting on it was rare and sporadic up to the middle of the 19th century, and its commercial exploitation was an unknown business until much later. The ancient Jews appear to have known nothing, of themselves, about the theatre or its implications in art and society; all that they did know seems to have been derived from the Greeks: their records, thus far, reveal, according to the learned, no native stage, no spontaneous and characteristic native drama. The literary forms conserved in the Bible are lyric, narrative, and aphoristically discursive, the forms of the songs and the psalms, the

3

histories and the novels, the prophecies and the "wisdom books."

The learned agree that all these contain dramatic potentialities; they deny that these potentialities were ever realized in intentional composition. Mr. Moulton suggests that this is due to the lack of a theatre, and attributes to this lack the spread of the obvious dramatic impulse of the Jews "through other literary forms, until epic, lyric, discourse, are all drawn together on a common basis of dramatic representation": for him hence, the Book of Job, the bulk of which is in dialogue form, is a complete and integrate composition, "a dramatic poem framed in an epic story," but not a drama. For Genung, Job is an "epic of the inner life," but not a drama; for Nathaniel Schmidt it is at most a dialogue, after the fashion of Plato, or more generously, of Æschylus in "Prometheus Bound," but not a drama. Most writers, in fact, who assign Job any dramatic character at all, attribute this character to Greek influence, and deny the nativity of dramatic form to Jewish soil. The position is, I think, incontrovertible. The only books in the Bible in which dialogue appears entirely for its own sake are Canticles and Job. But Canticles is known to be of very late origin and to bear striking resemblance to the poems of Theocritus, and Job, at first blush, anyhow, seems to have closer affinities with the discourses of the prophets and of the wise men, than with anything genuinely dramatic. Nathaniel Schmidt puts the reasons against considering Job a drama better than any one else I know of.

"The dialogues," he writes, "have caused some writers to describe this book as a drama. Insofar as the sentiments are not presented by the author in his own name, or as expressions of his own mental state, but put upon the lips of his heroes, as appropriate manifestations of their feelings and points of view, these speeches seem to have something of a dramatic nature. But a series of dialogues is not sufficient to constitute a drama. The most essential thing in this form of poetry is the progress of action; and in the dialogues of Job there is no action. So far as there is any progress of events in the book at all, it is exclusively found in the prose narration, partly prefaced and partly added to the dialogues. In the speeches of Job and his friends the situation is exactly the same from beginning to end. Even if there were such a thing as a drama of intellectual struggles not leading to any complications in life, it would still, to be a drama in any sense, have to reveal a progress of thought, a deepening plot of mental problems attacking the soul, and some solution. But there is no such advance from discourse to discourse, from cycle to cycle in these dialogues. The intellectual situation throughout is as unchanged as the external. The same ideas are repeated, with pleasing variety, to be sure, but without any appreciable movement of thought either toward a culminating point of mental bewilderment or in the direction of a final solution. It is true that the repetition itself and the variation give an increasing sense of the terrible character of the problem, and of all it involves, and also that there is a growing demand that the Most High shall justify his ways with Job. But of a dramatic complication and a real dénouement there is not the slightest trace. If it is argued that in " Prometheus Bound " there is, in a similar manner, a practically unchanged situation, with reflections from different points of view upon the hero's condition and what it signifies, and without a marked advance either in thought or action, it must be remembered that this drama only formed a part of a trilogy given at the same time, and that what little we know of the last two parts is sufficient to indicate in a general way the onward march of events.

" It is, in all probability, to . . . Greek influence that the dialogue form in Job is due. No sooner had the Greeks established themselves in Egypt or the Syrian cities than they built for themselves theatres and had performances of their great tragedies and comedies. Even those who never attended the theatre, or could not have understood the language, would be able to glean much information concerning the use of the building and what was done on the stage. The dialogue has been used for the purpose of presenting philosophic thought pre-eminently by a great Greek thinker, who was also a poet, Plato. The fact may well have been known, even though the dialogues of Plato had not been read. The greatest Semitic poet, by adopting this form, probably approached nearer to the drama, without reaching it, than any man of genius this family had produced." [1]

Such is the reasoning of those who believe that Job is not drama. What further lies behind it is the belief, based on the philological and other considerations, that the work of the great poet of Job is contained in only Chapters 3 to 31 inclusive; that of these, chapters 24 to 28 are interpolations and additions: that the speeches

[1] N. Schmidt: "The Messages of the Poets," p. 78 ff.: Scribner's.

of Yahweh may be such; as are also the descriptions of Behemoth and Leviathan, Chapters XL: 15 to XLI: 26. In all, by including the prose prologue and epilogue, no less than seven different hands are thus traceable in the Book of Job. Nevertheless, there is in the book, according to Dr. Schmidt, " a certain unity not seen in any other."

Now this unity is indubitable. The Greek influence is, I think, also beyond question. But this influence is, in my opinion, the influence neither of Plato nor of Æschylus; it is the influence of Euripides. And this unity is not an extraordinary accident, but the outcome, in the poetic total of Job, of a rigidly adhered to plan of composition. This plan I believe to be the typical one of the Euripidean tragedy, modified by the literary tradition and spiritual quality of the Jewish race into something new and different. In a word, we have in the Book of Job as it has come down to us, a Hebraized form of the Greek tragedy, with what may be the beginning and end of the legend or novel on which the drama was based attached to it, perhaps unchanged, perhaps altered to suit the necessary functions of prologue and epilogue they so obviously serve.

. . . The spiritual impulse expressed in the great social and ritual reformation under Josiah, which preceded the destruction of the first temple in Jerusalem, did not exhaust itself in the national disaster which followed almost immediately upon the enactment of Deuteronomy. It did not altogether lapse, nor was it completely spent in the social and religious readjustments required of the Jews by their *nidduch,* or exile from the land of their fathers. Its direction was some-

what changed; emphasis was shifted from social order
to ritual ordination, but it lived on, intensely, in the
prophets and the psalmists of this exile, and it ulti-
mately effected the restoration, the building of the second temple, the resurrection of the hopes of political
independence and power; and, when these failed and
Zerubbabel, the suffering servant of Yahweh, was removed, it effected the conversion of the community in
Palestiné into a central church, bearing in a sentimental
and vague and general way the same relation to the
other Jewish communities of the diaspora that Rome
bears to Catholicism of today. The Temple could be
in Jerusalem alone. Everywhere else, from the Nile to
the Ganges, from the Euxine Sea to the Persian Gulf,
the Jewish houses of worship were synagogues only;
the ultimate worship of Yahweh could take place nowhere save in Jerusalem. But these synagogues were
the meeting-houses and public studies of communities
which, however much diversified in speech, custom, commercial and political interests, were living a common
life according to the same specific laws and in the service
of the same specific ideals; communities, therefore, pos-
sessed of a social if not a racial homogeneity more
definite and more conspicuous than any in the orient or
occident of that day.

In affairs the members of these communities seem, on
the whole, to have been uniformly prosperous. They
were engaged in agriculture, in commerce, in banking;
the nobles among them were often in the favor, and
shared the responsibilities, of the imperial government
at the Persian capital and in the provinces. As a
people they were conspicuously self-conscious and

solidary. On the one side the pressure of social need and economic interest, on the other their religious separatism rendered them peculiarly sensitive to differences of cult and culture. The former compelled them to make use of the speech, the traditions and the social organization of the peoples among whom they sojourned. The latter required that they keep themselves ritually pure. Both necessities tended to evoke from them violent reactions of attraction or antipathy to views and policies of life other than their own. In this respect they were unique among Asiatic populations. The latter, always under the heel of an autocrat whose particular concern with them was to take from them as much and to give them as little as possible, had no conscious corporate interests, no definite and spontaneous corporate ideals. Conquerors might come and conquerors might go, they and the seasons went on forever. Who exploited them was to them a matter of indifference: Assyrian, Babylonian, Chaldean, Egyptian, Persian, Greek — were all one; exploited they were always, and nothing more. Hence the great empires were established and destroyed in two or three strokes; they were expressive of no great popular ideals and embodied no widespread popular interests. They were brigandage, not government, created by force, maintained by force and by force destroyed. They could not matter to their victims.

To this situation the Jews formed, as I have already indicated, a sole exception. Their natural race-life had come to consciousness in them first in religion, then in nationality, then in an identification of the two, and this identification had taken the typical form of the theory and practice of life, unique and with well-defined characteristics, which we call Hebraism. Hebraism became the inevitable standard of their judgment of both things of the flesh and things of the spirit, the basis of all acceptances and all rejections of the varied world that surrounded them. By its force their religion lived and endured; so that while other oriental religions were deglutinated into the eclectic mush of the times, Judaism, like Job who challenged its truth, clung to its integrity, and with all its borrowings from Babylonia, from Persia, from Greece, remained the same, not only not deformed by what it had borrowed, but much enriched.

The supreme test of its strength to endure, indeed, of the entire Jewish theory of life, came in its confrontation with the Greek spirit, with Hellenism. A connection, intimate and interpenetrative, was thereupon established which in its Christian forms is almost an identity. There is, in fact, beneath the overt divergences of the two visions fundamental likeness as well as fundamental difference. Greeks and Jews were the only peoples in the pre-Roman world who had historic sense and wrote histories; they were the only peoples who aimed at freedom consciously; they were the only peoples who turned natural literary forms into forms of art. But Jews looked outward, to the inscrutable powers of being that they called God; and Greeks looked inward to the intimate forms of human preference that they called " the Good." The different visions sprang from the same necessities and raised the same problems, but their expressions were different and their solutions were different. The latter, for the Jews, became *the fear of the Lord* which is the beginning of wisdom, while for the Greeks it is *the love of the Good* which is the beginning of wisdom. In the outcome, the Jews isolated man in the universe; " I know that he will slay me," says Job, " I have no hope. Yet will I maintain mine integrity before him ": while the Greeks made the spirit of man at home in the world, which is for them the substance of the good. In effect Hellenism was thus founded on an illusion, but a spontaneous and natural illusion, an illusion that made for the free self-expression of the human spirit. Hellenism is the gospel of Man, from the Greeks to all mankind, uttering, like Hebraism, the corporate life of a particular people, come to consciousness in the form of a specific practice and theory, at once a way of living and standard of judgment of good and of evil in all else.

Concerning Hellenism's nature and qualities the Greeks were even prouder than the Jews were of Hebraism, and they were as exclusively racial, though not so particularistic. To them their gospel was a mission. They reinforced and accelerated the original expansive powers of the Greek vision, which immediately fascinated every mentality that encountered it, with attempts at reconstructing the conquered barbarian world according to the Greek model. Alexander, the Seleucidæ and Ptolemies were Hellenizers. That they passed on the mere shell of Hellenism is incidental to their intent. In fact, they intended the impossible. The Hellenization was a change of external form, not of inward spirit, and it could be nothing else. A theory of life is the culmination of a long racial experience, recorded and studied; incorporated first in cult, tradition, and custom, then in conscious social organization in the arts, in letters, in philosophy. It is the flowering and fruitage of a particular kind of family tree and springs from a specific root. To Hellenize, therefore, or to Hebraize, is nothing more than to make general the mere forms and shells of Greek or Jewish life and thought. The spirit can not be transplanted and diffused, nor can it become operative in the body politic of other people, for spirit is a function of time, first of all and most deeply of all, and then of place and circumstance. Thus, in the Hellenistic world, the great masses remained unmoved, changed in neither temper nor outlook; by no stretch of the imagination can they be thought of as Greeks; while for the classes, Hellenism was merely the refinement of their own particular modes of life. That there were many individual exceptions goes without saying — like the legendary Jew whom Aristotle met and found Greek not only in speech but in spirit! Hellenists in spirit are born at all times and in all places: outside of Hellas, however, they are sports, not types; they are not true-bred to their stock, and do not survive.

The first encounter of Jews and Greeks, the one a people fixed inexorably upon maintaining unaltered their divinely-ordained mode of life, the other a people determined to establish their own forms for all mankind, could, nevertheless, have been nothing else than friendly. Most of the Jews were in exile, by choice perhaps, but in exile, and looking to the rebuilding of a holy city and an only Temple, looking to a unique and unpicturable God for inspiration and spiritual sustenance. They were to be found in communities like Elephantine, where they lived lives that embittered Jeremiah. They were to be found in Syrian towns ruled by Persian satraps, themselves in the service of the Persians even in the Greek Asiatic colonies the latter had conquered. The Greeks, again, were retaliating in force. Thucydides speaks of an Athenian army of occupation that spent ten years in Egypt, and contacts of Greek colonials and Ionian merchants with Jews in Syria were inevitable. Later, under the imaginative guidance of the young Alexander, the Greeks were entering upon a march of battle through uncharted lands. Both they and the Jews were then sojourners in foreign countries, surrounded by enemies. That the Jews, a united and solidary people, whose communities ranged along trade's highroad from Egypt to India, could be of great assistance to the Greeks goes without saying. They were, perhaps, the most widely-known race of Alexander's day. They alone, of all peoples, had direct and friendly communication with the seaboard. Their contention, hence, that Alexander from the beginning favored them, that he granted them civic rights and privileges in his city of Alexandria and throughout his empire, has everything in its favor. It is known that his policy was continued by the Seleucids at Seleucia and Antioch and by the Ptolemies at Alexandria. In the interval between the end of the fifth and the end of the second century B. C. E. Greeks and Jews were in friendly contact throughout the cities of the Hellenistic world.

Now the cities of the Hellenistic world, in form at least, were Hellenic cities. Those which Alexander or his successors built were naturally constituted after the Greek mode; but also the ancient Syrian cities they conquered and favored were reformed, and their amorphous oriental organization was replaced by the organic Athenian constitution. The reconstruction stopped short only at Jerusalem. Even its ancient rival and near neighbor, Samaria, repeopled with Macedonians, was governed in the Greek way and continued for many years in this way, side by side with the holy city of the Jews, without overt enmity or too much friction. Its Hellenic character was expressed, however, not alone in its form of government. The most adequate embodiment of Hellenism came in the three great Greek civic institutions — the gymnasium, the hippodrome, and the theatre. No Hellenized city was without these.

Gymnasia and theatres were the important institutions of the three. The former, intended especially for the training of powerful fighting men, became, under the varying fortunes of history, social centers. They were headquarters of associations of young men, not very different from the student societies of all times. These associations were called epheboi. Their members wore a particular type of tunic and cap and enjoyed a predominant share in those celebrations and festivals which express so adequately the unity of Greek city life. It was the introduction, into Jerusalem, of a gymnasium with all, in the social order, that it implied, which is noted by the pious historian of I Maccabees as the beginning of the momentous Maccabean struggle. "In those days," he writes, "there came forth out of Israel transgressors of the law and persuaded many. . . . And they built a place of exercise in Jerusalem according to the laws of the Gentiles; and they made themselves uncircumcised and forsook the holy covenant, and joined themselves to the Gentiles and sold themselves to evil." According to the supplementary account of II Maccabees, the evil seems to have consisted in forming " a body of youths to be trained " in the " place of exercise," in wearing the " Greek hat," in developing the extreme Greek fashions and in " thinking the glories of the Greeks best of all." This was the culmination of a long and silent process in which the constant and intimate communication between the Jews of the diaspora, particularly of Alexandria, and the Jews of Jerusalem played a chief rôle. In point of fact it would have been endured and assimilated by Jerusalem, and after a while, cherished. Without the intolerable demands of Antiochus Epiphanes, his profanation and robbery of the temple, the Hellenization of Jerusalem would insofar forth have been as peaceable and fruitful, if not so rapid, as the Hellenization of the other communities, in what survived of Alexander's empire. The significant thing is that the process complained of in Maccabees was not sudden, but a gradual thing which presupposes a long familiarity with things Greek among Jerusalem Jews.

The historian of Maccabees makes mention only of the gymnasium, and it may be that the Hellenizing party built no theatre in Jerusalem. Whether one ever existed there only archæological investigations can show. The other cities of the Hellenistic world, however, would have been felt to be incomplete without their theatres. Ruined remains of them are to be found everywhere. They were the places not alone for stage-performances, but also for public gatherings and popular assemblies. Often, companies of actors were at-

tached to them and where these were not maintained by
the kings or the cities themselves, performances were
given by strolling players, " artists attached to the god
Dionysus." Dionysia were to be found everywhere in
the Hellenistic world: from the days of Xenophon to
those of Antiochus Epiphanes the Jews of the diaspora,
if not those of Palestine, must have been familiar with
the theatre and theatrical performances.

Now among the Jews of the diaspora Hellenization
met with no particular hindrances. Before the coming of the Greeks their speech had been for generations
not Hebrew but Aramaic. The replacing of Aramaic
by Greek was a matter of little time. To the great and
powerful community in Alexandria, however Jewish in
practice and belief, Hebrew had become at the end of
a hundred years an unknown tongue. It could not
serve even as the sacred language of the sacred books,
and to keep those accessible to the Greek-speaking community necessitated that series of translations of the
Pentateuch into Greek, known as the Septuagint. This
event, which took perhaps twice a hundred years to
culminate, was the beginning of a series of such translations of Hebrew books into Greek, the most definitely
dated being the translation of Ecclesiasticus by the
grandson of its author, in the seventh or eighth decade
of the second century B. C. E.

Alexandrian Jewry of the third and second century
B. C. E., did not, however, confine its literary activity
to translation. Spiritual leadership in the Hellenistic
world had passed from Athens to Alexandria, and
though that city did not receive the Greek soul, it
emulated and cherished and imitated the perfect forms

in which that soul had had its perfect expression. The library and museum failed, perhaps, to stimulate the creative imagination, but they sheltered and encouraged scholarship, and if they housed no great poets, they fostered talented men of letters. The spiritual change from *Hellenic* to *Hellenistic* is marked by what, for want of a better term, may be called the academic quality, the smell of the library in contrast with the fragrance of life. Art and thought looked backward rather than lived forward. The period is one of reproduction, not of creation. The Greeks imitated their own classics and the rest of the world imitated the Greeks. The Jews felt it a shame not to do likewise, and some generations after Alexander tried, even by forgeries, to prove how Greek they were. In Alexandria they developed, spontaneously, a Judæo-Greek literature which became more and more important as Hellenistic culture properly so called decayed. They reproduced in Greek forms the specific content of their own vision and they Hellenized it so far as they could in history, in philosophy, in epic poetry and in drama. Eusebius quotes three small fragments of an epic poem on Jerusalem, by one Philo, not the great philosopher Philo; he cites a long poem by one Theodotus on the history of the town of Sichem, and both he and Clement of Alexandria speak of Ezekiel, "the poet of Jewish tragedies," and cite one of his plays, dealing with the Exodus and based on the Biblical narrative.

This play, probably one among many, was written, says Schuerer, who is the authoritative student of the period, to acquaint the Hellenized Jews with the Bible story and to provide a Jewish alternative for the too attractive Gentile entertainments. Its verses are prosaic, although diction and metre are fluent. From the fragments preserved by Clement and Eusebius it may be gathered that the action of the play opens with a long monologue by Moses, who has just fled to Midian to escape the consequences of his having killed the Egyptian taskmaster. The monologue tells the story of his life and mourns his fate in having to become a wanderer in a foreign land. This over, the seven daughters of Raguel appear, Zipporah, in answer to his questions making known to him who and what they are. Thereupon the flocks are watered and Zipporah and Moses are married. In the second extract Moses relates a dream to his father-in-law, and the latter interprets it as meaning that Moses is destined to high place and to knowledge of things past, present and future.

In the third extract the Epiphany occurs: Yahweh's voice comes to Moses from the burning bush, commissioning him to deliver the children of Israel out of Egyptian bondage. The details of the Epiphany and the speech of Yahweh follow the narrative of Exodus closely. The subsequent citation repeats the situation, if not the scene, Yahweh giving in it more exact directions concerning the departure from Egypt and the celebration of the Passover.

The next citation shows the deliverance accomplished. An Egyptian of Pharaoh's host, who alone has escaped death in the Red Sea, gives an account of how the Jews crossed it, how the Egyptians pursued them, how the catastrophe came. The account, modified by much specification of detail, is a close restatement of the narrative of Exodus.

The last citation takes us to the Israelitish camp in the wilderness. A messenger brings to Moses the news of an excellent place of encampment near Elim, with twelve springs of water and seventy palm trees. He adds a circumstantial account of the observation of a wonderful, mighty bird, twice as large as an eagle, followed in its flight, as their king, by the whole feathered tribe.

The familiar features of Euripidean construction stand out even in this synopsis — the recapitulative prologue, the epiphany, the forecast of the future. No doubt has arisen that this play conformed completely to the Euripidean model and falls within the Euripidean tradition. No doubt could arise. The school of Euripides is the only school of Hellenistic tragedy; the work of Euripides is the great outstanding dramatic influence in the Hellenic no less than in the Hellenistic world.

§ 2. *Job and the Euripidean Tradition.*

The vogue and influence of Euripides constitute an almost unparalleled fact in literary history. His lifetime is practically coincident with the Golden Age and decadence of Athens (485 to 406 B. C. E.). His influence is coincident with the prevalence of Hellenism in the world of antiquity. It is not so much the profundity of his thought, the clarity and beauty of his expression, the vigorous yet subtle character of his broader dramatic craftsmanship, that keep his hold on the imagination of those who lived after him so unique.

In that respect he shares glory with the other mighty poets and thinkers of his age. It is that these qualities should have been so tremendous as to turn an alien dramaturgic convention into a dramatic standard, through all the while that drama was written in the ancient world. Like his fellows in the unmatched Athenian trinity, Æschylus and Sophocles, he had written innumerable dramas. But where we possess only seven each from the hands of the other two, we possess nineteen from the hand of Euripides, besides countless fragments to which excavations are continually adding. It is from Euripides that Plato and Aristotle most constantly quote; him that Aristophanes cannot let alone. It is he who is called the " most tragical of the poets," so admired of Socrates that the latter would go to the theatre for the performance of no other. It is he who is the beloved of the Athenian intellectuals of the fifth century and the hated and feared of the demagogues and conservatives. From his works the Hellenistic teachers chose their models of tragic poetry; his work it was they edited for ordinary reading in schools. Vase painters and actors of pantomime selected their themes from it. Even six hundred years after his death it was performed, and before enthusiastic audiences. His example set style, theme and form for tragedy so long as the ancients wrote it. Indeed, if we may trust Aristophanes (Frogs 99), during his very lifetime the younger writers imitated him, while the dramatic writers of the fourth century knew no other model, and Roman tragedies were measured by no other standards.

That, in spite of the appreciation of the intellectuals,

he was a prophet without honor in his own country, is a commonplace. How with only four exceptions, he invariably came off second or third best in the great civic competitions, how he was a butt for the comic writers, how false and scandalous stories were circulated about his life, his family, his opinions and even his death, in exile in a strange land — these are things that every schoolboy knows. But readers of Lucian may also recall the story that he tells of the men of Abdera in Thrace, so obsessed by Euripides' Andromeda, that they went about the streets entranced, murmuring to themselves " O Love, high monarch over gods and men —" And readers of Plutarch may recall how, after the battle of Carrhae, a certain marriage-festival was celebrated by a performance of the Bacchae in which the head of Crassus figured. In the Hellenistic world, wherever a company of players was to be found, whatever city maintained a theatre, there one or more plays by Euripides was in the repertory, there at each Dionysia one or more performances of a Euripidean tragedy took place. In truth, at the beginning of the fourth century Euripides is known and played wherever Greek communities are to be found; by its end he is the only member of the ancient trinity whose work still holds the stage and holds it not only as a part of the regular repertory, but as a favorite in the theatre, so much so that the tragedies of his imitators cannot rival his in popular regard.

This was as true in Egypt where the Jews were numerous and strong as elsewhere in the Hellenistic world. The plays of Euripides quite held their own with the works of his Alexandrian followers, and this

so late as the third century and in face of the fact that
the Alexandrian theatre had through the munificence
and patronage of the second Ptolemy, who reigned
from 285 to 247, become the most famous in the world,
with the most liberal prizes and the most numerous
contests, the competitors being the best poets and actors of the time.

Now it was during the reign of this Ptolemy that
the Jews of Alexandria discovered that they had become so Hellenized in speech as to need a Greek version
of their holy writ. According to the legend it was
his patronage that initiated the miraculous Septuagint
which is the traditional beginning of Judæo-Greek literature. In point of fact, the Septuagint was probably the last step in a series of translations that had
been needed and initiated many generations earlier,
and that point to a century-long acquaintance with
Greek speech, and by implication with Greek life and
art. The coincidence of this indication of the complete Hellenization of Alexandrian Jews, in speech at
least, with the most brilliant period of the Alexandrian
drama is significant. Willy-nilly, the Jews must for
generations have seen the processions, the performances,
the competitions; willy-nilly, they must have been impressed and fascinated and eager for more, so much so
that in another generation they have at least one
tragedian of their own, who writes tragedies about their
own legendary heroes, and according to Euripidean
standards of form.

Ezekiel of Alexandria, the learned say, was an effective play-wright of more than one play. Is it con-
ceivable that his should be the one unique sporadic

attempt at dramatic writing in the whole history of Hebraic literature in all its languages? That the form he used should have no sanction in the sacred books themselves? Such a conception runs counter the probabilities; literary, like biological types occur in species, not uniquely, and the Jews evoked and found authority and models in their sacred books for everything they undertook in the field of the spirit. In Hebrew as well as in Greek, there must have been imitations prior to Ezekiel's imitations; clumsy and blundering at first, no doubt, skill-less and amateurish, but imitations adhering, so far as the conditions allowed, definitely to the outlines of the Euripidean tragic form.

What was this form, and how did the author of Job, living probably toward the end of the fifth century, get knowledge of it? In any specific sense the latter half of this question is impossible to answer. He may have heard of it from an Egyptian or Syrian Jew visiting Palestine; a returned Palestinian traveller may himself have seen a play of Euripides enacted, in Egypt in the Athenian camp, or in some coastal Syrian city, or elsewhere. Suppose he did, how much of it could he have carried away with him? All, if he were familiar with Greek; the bare form if he were not. Whether he was familiar with Greek no one can say: there are very few Hellenisms in the text of Job, and those in suspected portions, while the intent of Job is distinctly untraditional and Euripidean. It shows an intimate familiarity with the Hebraic tradition such as was natural to one of the *hakamim* or wise men, together with a keen conception of its weaknesses. It is in a given sense a challenge and a defiance of the orthodox content of that tradition, even while maintaining it formally. It bears a relation to Jewish orthodoxy extraordinarily like that of so many of the plays of Euripides to Greek orthodoxy. How, now, might so distinctively Hebraic a work receive the Hellenic form?

Here is one way, as plausible as any other. Imagine our author on a visit to Egypt or the Syrian coast, where Greeks live and Persians rule, a passionate humanist among the wise, seeing the wonders of the cities under the guidance of one of his brethren from the Jewish community, and perhaps himself only just enough acquainted with the Greek to catch the drift of what he hears, to retain its generic essence, but to miss the ardent and varied life of it, much as might an American in France, ill-acquainted with French. Imagine him present, alone or with his guide, during one of the great festivals at a performance of Bacchae or Orestes or Bellerophontes or any other of the favorite dramas of the period. What would he see, and hear, and what, under such circumstances, would most stand out in his uncloyed mind?

First of all, he would hear the prologue. He would note its narrative form of solemn and terse restatement of legendary material, its function of preparing the way for the drama that is to follow, its orthodoxy, and the perhaps supernatural character of the speaker of it.

Then, as the drama developed, he would note its radical difference in tone and thought from the prologue, the frequent violent contrasts between the senti-

ments of all the protagonists and those of the prologue. The body of the play would strike him as
heterodox. Now the heterodoxy would be most prominent in the long set speeches of the agon where, besides, he might catch more definitely the profundity of
the thought and the quality of the feeling. Knowing
nothing of the historic and ritual basis of the drama
and its form, he would not distinguish the leader of
the chorus from the other protagonists: he would take
him to be a fourth actor, sharing the dialogue with
the other three, but he would hardly identify him, or
her, as the leader of the chorus. Again, he would be
particularly struck, by the appearance, at the crisis
of the play, of a new character, not formerly mentioned, an appearance perhaps altogether unannounced.
Upon the very long discourse of this character much
of the subsequent action might depend. In the Greek
drama this character is called the messenger. In
Euripides his speech is always the longest, he always
tells of past disaster or bodings of disaster to come,
and he often gives advice.

Most of all our playgoer would be struck by the appearance and rôle of the *deus ex machina*. Even
Aristotle remarked that Euripides used this Epiphany
of God to bring to a conclusion the much entangled
action of a play, as in the Hippolytus or Orestes or
Helen. A stranger unfamiliar with the language and
legend of the drama might, therefore, hardly be cul-
pable for thinking the same. And if he saw, besides,
the work of the later tragedians, he would be justified
in regarding the function of the *deus* to be solely this.
He would, however, observe that the god, after hav-

ing untied the dramatic knot, assumed the character of a narrative epilogue foretelling the future of the personages, ordaining the ritual whence the tragedy derives, the worship of the divinity in whose honor it was written. He would note, in a word, that the ending of a Euripidean drama is as narrative and orthodox as its beginning.

Finally there is the chorus, always present on the stage, capable of interfering with the action yet rarely doing so, expressing itself chiefly in song, song that gives voice to orthodox sentiment, to ornate description of legendary events and objects, to emotional commentary on the action. A stranger would be much struck by this, and by the duplicity of its function and the incongruities that gave rise to. For the chorus would sometimes also interfere with the action, and never to any effect.

§ 3. *The Literary Form of the Book of Job.*

Now conceive our hakam returned to Palestine, stirred as many another Jew had been and was to be, by " the glories of the Greeks." Poet that he was, the temptation to make use of this new and effective form must have been irresistible. There is a startling nearness, a painful immediacy in Job's description of suffering that can rise from no vicariousness, no sympathy, no mere force of imagination. It is the poet's soul itself that has been hurt, and that has conquered its hurt. In the traditional forms of his own literature there are utterances of complaint, of piteous prayer, of faith, of hope. But there were no traditional forms which gave voice to doubt, to accusation, to defiance. The different mood demanded a different form, and the dramatic form was ready to hand and welcome. His essay at dramatic writing could hardly have resulted in anything more successful than Job. Our poet was a hakam, completely, if we may trust his text, the child of the Hebraic tradition, with its myth and magic as well as its wisdom woven into the very substance of his mind. The use of mythological material is indeed greater in Job than in any other of the wisdom books of the Bible, or in the prophets, just as it was strongly marked in the dramas of Euripides. I cannot help thinking that it is the dramatic form that makes the poet bring this material into the foreground. It is a form which causes the long and lyrical utterances of prophets and psalmists to stand out, and the disputations of the schools. The poet is much more interested, one gathers from the study of it, in precept and idea than in action; what would be central for him would thus naturally be the agon. And the other elements of the Euripidean drama would be so modified in terms of the Hebraic temperament and literary tradition, that there would be at once the form without the substantial plot-construction of that drama, and such corrections of the form as would obviously suggest themselves. The most important of these would be the modification of the function of the chorus, so that it became absolutely detached from the action and acquired completely the character of a didactically lyrical interlude in commentary. Euripides himself, no less than the generation succeeding

Euripides' had made such modifications. So also the author of Job.

Thus, like the Greek tragedies, Job consists of the dramatic treatment of an ancient legend. It has a prologue which tells as swiftly and deftly as the Euripidean prologue all that precedes the opening of the action. It gives the orthodox preliminary version of the legend. That its form is prose, even the very prose of the ancient written legend, offers no difficulties. For, beside the swifter and profounder verse of the dramatic dialogue, the Euripidean prologues also must in utterance have had the effect of prose, particularly to foreign hearers. The poet could well have let this portion of the legend stand unchanged as prologue, and did.

After the prologue comes the drama itself. It is complained that nothing happens. But from the poet's point of view the dialogue is the happening; it culminates in the challenge of the justice of God. In form it has the characteristics of the Euripidean *agon*. The speeches are set, argumentative, and however tense with emotion, always within the bounds of the literary methods of the " wisdom books." They are in verse, almost exclusively tetrastichs, and there are four speakers who argue in succession, like Helen and Hecuba before Menelaus.

The movement of the dialogue is significant; its climax, from the standpoint of the orthodox Jew of the period, terrible. Job makes the opening speech. His suffering, he declares, has brought him to the breaking-point; he can endure no more and begs for death. Eliphaz, the oldest of the three friends who have come to comfort him, tries to console him by advising him patience. Suffering, he asserts, Polonius-like, is the inevitable lot of man. The just and omnipotent God who sent the ill, will send good also, a thousandfold. But Job can find no comfort in this advice. He has asked his friends for nothing and sees no relief in the patience they advise. Life, he feels, grows only more and more unendurable; all he begs is the mere relief of death. Such a prayer, the pompous Bildad finds, is sin, for it accuses God of injustice. But God forever sends harm to the wicked only. Let Job but wait, and his lost prosperity shall return to him. Job acknowledges " that it is so." But God is too mighty and elusive to be stayed for by mere man. As man he is compelled to say " He destroyeth the perfect with wicked." He wants no more than a little peace before death. This makes Zophar, who appears to be a dogmatic, impatient man of middle age, very angry. How dare Job call himself " perfect! " In fact, omnipotence is punishing him for sin, and less than he deserves. If only Job would be humble and acknowledge his sinfulness, his prosperity would return. To which Job retorts that he knows as much about God as his friends know, and declares flatly that God is unjust and hurts the righteous man without cause.

In the second round of the dialogue Eliphaz declares that misfortune comes to the wicked only, and just implies that Job might be of their class. Job appeals from him and the other two to God, who is torturing him without reason, hinting that they and not he deserve the torture; whereto Bildad retorts that Job is actually undergoing punishment for his crimes, and provokes Job to the declaration that God had wronged him, and that these, his would-be comforters, are wronging him, but that his " avenger liveth and shall stand up at the last upon earth." To this Zophar replies that from " of old time " only the wicked have suffered and perished. Whereupon Job demonstrates that, on the contrary, the wicked are prospered and die in peace.

Eliphaz begins the third phase of the dialogue by pointing out that man alone can gain anything by righteousness and that Job, being in disaster, has been guilty of such and such crimes. He begs Job to turn to God and be saved. But though Job would gladly turn to God, Job cannot find him. He knows himself to be faultless and would prove it so to the Almighty who alone tortures him and makes him afraid. Bildad thereupon suggests that God is too infinite to be known; what we know is a " small whisper; and the thunder of his power, who can understand? " But of what use is an unreachable God to a despairing man, cries Job. In the name of that same God he holds fast his righteousness " and will not let it go. My heart shall not reproach me so long as I live." Whereto Zophar retorts sharply that none the less, Job's condition shows that he is unrighteous. In final refutation Job contrasts what he was with what he is, giving an account of his whole life and then challenging God's wrath if there be any blemish in it —" Lo here is my signature — let God reply! "

The situation at the end of this agon must have been, from the point of view of orthodox Jewry, intolerable. The mood of Job has changed in the course of the dialogue from unhappy complaint to heroic defiance. The argument has moved from the position that (1) God sends undeserved misfortune on the righteous, through the demonstration that (2) he deals prosperity to the wicked, to the final position that (3) an omnipotent and unattainable God is of no use to the just man who suffers, and who demands that God shall justify himself. The friends have grown weaker as Job has grown stronger. From argument they have passed to iteration. The intellectual and emotional situation at the end is the reverse of the situation at the beginning.

Now it is in this situation that Elihu appears. Critics have called his speeches interpolations by a later and inferior writer. But why should they appear just where they do appear? It was not, to use Dr. Schmidt's phrase, more " natural " to put them there, than to put them after chapter 30. Their " lateness " is based partly on the textual observation that Aramaic and Greek terms appear in them; and Siegfried has shown that also many of the descriptions of God in the text of the dialogue have their parallel in psalms of the Maccabean era, and that the text itself contains late Hebrew words, Aramaisms and Arabisms. It does not, however, follow from this that the speech is entirely an interpolation by a different hand. It may be only a modification and prolongation by a different hand, or a rewriting by a different hand. Its appearing where it does has a dramatic propriety which of itself indicates some familiarity with the Greek drama. That it partly recapitulates the argument is no reason for considering it an inferior interpolation. It adds something also. And it has precedent in many of the messenger's speeches in Greek plays, which tell the audience what they already know. Moreover the recapitulation is not the essential burden of Elihu's speech. Its burden is that the defense of God by the friends has failed. And this is bad news. Its burden is the registry of that fact and the warning to Job against his pride of opinion. Its burden is more particularly to announce what has happened and what is to come. Most notably the speeches of Elihu lead up to and prepare for the speeches of Yahweh. Elihu's rôle, in a word, is that of a messenger. He appears, an ardent youth, compelled to speak by inward stress, for God, who reveals himself in visions, through suffering, who is overwhelmingly just and will manifest himself in answer to Job's challenge when he is ready; who always delivers those who submit to his just, merciful and inscrutable will; whose majesty is revealing itself in the storm that is arising, in the golden splendor out of the north; "who cometh with a terrible majesty upon him."

And God comes as announced, a whirlwind and a voice. The Hebrew convention about images made it impossible that God should assume any form. His presence could be nothing else than a voice, out of the burning bush in Ezekiel's "Exodus," out of the whirlwind, in the dialogue of Job. There is no less reason for regarding this speech as interpolation than for regarding Elihu's speech as such. Neither does it, according to the more radical critics, add anything to the dialogue, which has "ended with the words of Job." But it is not necessary that it should add anything to the dialogue. Job has been demanding that God should confront him, has been complaining of his elusiveness. At the very time when Job seems absolute victor over his friends God appears, accepting Job's challenge and ready to enter into judgment with Job if the latter will. God's speech is either irrelevant iteration or profound subtlety: but what justifies the opinion that it is iteration? Nothing that I can see but the failure to think God's speech in terms of the dramatic development of the theme and its function as Epiphany. Closer scrutiny of its content than the learned seem to have made will show that God gives a very different account of himself than do his defenders in the dialogue. They emphasize his power, particularly in punishing wickedness, Job his indifference in prospering wickedness: he emphasizes his providence, particularly in maintaining the reasonless and helpless forms of life. Creator who has set bounds to the sea, made the world habitable, ordained the life-giving waters, controlled the stars, directed the lightning, he supplies the lion's whelp with food, superintends the travail of the hind of the wild goat, protects the wild ass and the wild ox, gives the war-horse strength, ordains the safe hatching of the ostrich egg, and maintains the hawk and the eagle in their ways. Such is God. If thou, Job, art like him, " array thyself with excellency and dignity." Abase the proud and punish the wicked and I will acknowledge that thine own hand can save thee.

What can Job answer? He has demanded that God in kindness confront him in judgment. God appears, not, however without his terrors. Job is satisfied.

Behold, I am of small account, what can I answer thee?
I lay my hand upon my mouth:
Once I have spoken — I will not speak again;
Yea twice: I will proceed no further:

  And again:

I know that thou canst do all things
And that no purpose of thine can be restrained.
I have spoken, but without understanding,
Things too wonderful, which I did not know.
Only by hearsay had I known thee,
But now mine eye seeth thee,
And I recant my words, am comforted
Amid dust and ashes.

Thus God accomplishes what Eliphaz and Zophar
and Bildad could not accomplish. Job is comforted by
the knowledge of an everlasting and impartial providence in nature in which man has only a negligible
part, but a part. The Epiphany, as in the Euripidean
drama, saves an intolerable situation, so far as in the
course of nature it can be saved at all.

Then follows the epilogue in prose; perhaps, but by
no means certainly, the conclusion of the old prose
legend, and kept prose for the same reasons as the
prologue. Note how generally close in content it is
to the epilogue of the Euripidean tragedy — the or-
dainment of a ritual, the account of the future of the
chief protagonist. The drama closes in as Euripidean
a manner as it begins.

But where, in all this, is the most prominent mark of
Greek tragedy — the chorus? To answer this question
we may best, Yankee-wise, ask another one. Suppose
that an editor unacquainted with dramatic form or

knowing it to be connected with the worship of a strange
God and believing it to be anathema, had a Hebrew
play to deal with which he admired and wished to save,
what would he do with the choric songs, these being
most explicitly ritual in form and intent? What could
he do, save incorporate them into the dialogue, at such
places where, in his judgment, they fell or fitted? Now
the choruses mark the division of Greek tragedies into
" acts: " and there are usually four or five acts sep-
arated off from each other by choric songs. We
should therefore naturally expect the choruses to come
at the completion of each round of the dialogue, which
falls clearly into three rounds, or " acts " and is succeeded by the closing " acts " of the epiphany. Job
is a play in four acts. The choruses, if it has any, will
be distinguished from the dialogue by a difference in
metrical form or in theme, or in both. They should
have the character of didactic commentary on the dialogue or the action: they should be in a different di-
mension without being irrelevant, and they should be
three in number.

Now, it happens that Job contains three " interpolations " that satisfy these requirements. Two of these
occur in the " third act," the first, in the twenty fourth
chapter, is assigned to Job. It consists of a series of
descriptions of four typically wicked and criminal
classes and their ultimate fate at the hands of God.
It is written in tristichs, and tristichs are not stanzaic
units of the dialogue. The second occurs in the twenty-
eighth chapter. It is written in four strophes of three
tetrastichs each, with a refrain of the same distich.
Its theme is the elusiveness of wisdom, as creative

power, to man and the absolute possession of this creative power by God. The third is the description of Behemoth and Leviathan, the mightiest of God's creatures, attached to the speech of Yahweh, Chapters XL: 15–XLI: 26. This is written in the metre of the dialogues but is very different in theme and content. The animals it describes are creatures of imagination, not reality, like the Greek Chimera and Dionysian bull. Leviathan " is king over all the sons of pride."

If these are merely interpolations it is a very extraordinary coincidence that they should be three in number, that their themes should fall so pat to the changes of theme in the dialogues, and that two at least should be so different from the dialogue in metre or form. Their nature is generically so like that of many of the Euripidean choruses that it is more plausible than not that they are such. The poem on wisdom belongs clearly at the end of the first " act " in which Job and his friends have been accusing each other of ignorance concerning God. The natural choric comment should be what we find it to be, that men cannot attain wisdom, which is an attribute of God alone. The stanzas dealing with the typical evil doers and their fate come naturally at the end of the second " act." This act has discussed the fate of the unrighteous, the friends insisting that they perish unhappily and Job that they prosper to the end. The last " interpolation " seems to me to belong properly before the speech of Elihu. For Job's orthodox friends, God's justice is identical with his power. Job's inflexible self-justification and challenge to God can be met only with an exhibition of that power. The choric description of Behemoth and Leviathan are pat to that purpose, and have something of the Euripidean irony. For it is to be followed by the duly announced coming of God himself. Job is to have his wish and enter into judgment with the Almighty. It is distinctly a Euripidean touch to express in the chorus the impossibility of such a competition by the choric description of the terrible beasts which are the mere creatures of God and beside either of whom Job is a bubble.

With this the restoration of Job is complete. Prologue, *agon*, messenger, choruses, epiphany, epilogue, they are all evident with just those differences from the Greek that may be expected from the difference in tradition and background between the two authors. That the thought of Job has Euripidean analogues need not be argued. The injustice of divinity, the unhappiness of mankind, the desirability of death, the rebellion and the ultimate or primal mystical perception which consoles,— these are the commonplaces of Euripides' thinking. One play of Euripides, indeed, of which unhappily only fragments have survived to us, is in story and expression not unlike Job. It is Bellerophontes, completed in 425. The hero has lost his son at the hands of Ares, his daughter at those of Artemis. He too finds evil-doers to be prosperous, the weak oppressed by the strong. He doubts therefore that the gods exist, he strives to ascend to heaven that his doubts may be set at rest and he is blasted by a thunderbolt. Condemned by God but " clinging to his integrity," he wanders, lamed and blinded, over the face of the earth. His mood, as far as it may be gathered from a fragment (311) is very like that of Job. I use Mr. Murray's translation:

> " Reverent wast thou to God, had he but known,
> Thy door oped to the stranger, and thine help
> For them that loved thee knew no weariness."

PART II

THE JOBAN PHILOSOPHY OF LIFE

II

§ 1. *Job and the " Problem of Evil."*

However one may date the different parts of the Joban tragedy, they possess, bar the speech of Elihu, an interdependence which makes one part meaningless without the other. Prologue and epilogue certainly do not stand alone, and the dialogue proper, with all its unity, would hardly be intelligible without the prose setting. Even if the unity of the composition be only that of a mosaic rather than of an organism, it is a unity such as alone conscious attention could define and a generating purpose create. The meaning of Job, hence, is not to be sought in the dialogue alone nor in its setting alone. What meaning it has is of the whole, and in the whole. Nor can it be a merely intrinsic meaning. All works of art have intrinsic meanings, but their origin and life is not in those; their origin and life is in the historic situation which gave them rise. For a work of art is the effect of no detached individuality in an artist, of no isolated creative impulse bursting like a rocket into the course of history and flashing out again. The most individual of artists has a social setting, and his ideals, his perspective and his outlook are the expression of his reaction to his setting. They fail of significance without it, are mere color, mere noise, like

41

any other natural existence. Job is, of course, no exception.

The commonplace, therefore, that the theme of Job is the " problem of evil," needs to be reinterpreted and re-expressed. There is no absolute problem of evil any more than there is an absolute Man. Problems are functions of history, time, place and personality. If Job asks: Why does the just and good human being suffer, when there is an omnipotent God who also is just and good? his question has an occasion, in place and time, a root and growth in history and a refraction in the personal experience and character of the author. Concerning the last we know nothing; there is only what we can gather from the texture of his work, its fervor and its vision. Concerning the other things we must speculate, but we possess data from which the speculation can start, and by which its direction can be determined and its movement controlled.

For the bald Joban problem there exist the commonplace bald solutions, each arrived at by way of restating one or another of the positions developed by the agonists of the tragedy. Of such solutions one stresses the implication of the prologue and epilogue that suffering is purely a test of righteousness, a test which the righteous man triumphantly sustains. Another formulates into a single proposition the opinions of Eliphaz, Bildad and Zophar that suffering is retribution for sin: it reiterates the circular argument which Job so bitterly scorns, that since God is just and punishes only injustice, he who suffers must be unjust, and conversely, since a man suffers only when he is sinful, God is just and punishes only injustice. Still another, much more rarely, will restate Job's conviction that happiness and suffering are nothing necessary in relation to human conduct, that they come indifferently and perversely to both the righteous and the wicked. In this opinion, it is to be noted, Yahweh, after responding to Job's challenge by revealing his uncoercible omnipotence and thereby comforting him where his friends had only deepened his distress, is made in the epilogue to concur: "And it came to pass, after Yahweh had spoken these words unto Job, that Yahweh said unto Eliphaz the Temanite, mine anger is kindled against thee and thy two friends: for ye have not spoken of me the thing which is right, as my servant Job hath."

Of the traditional solutions, each carries its own implications concerning the nature of God and the character and destiny of man. For a solution of the "problem of evil" must be a theory of life, a theory which will define evil's proper place in the economy of nature and the flux of human enterprise. To seek a solution merely in the stated purposes of suffering is therefore not really to seek one at all. If one exists it will be found in the implications of such theories, implications metaphysical and moral, delineating the power that acts and the passion that suffers. For evil is a relation between man and his environment; its import derives from the nature of these, and from nothing else beside. Purposes are secondary to the being that wills the purposes, and it is too easy to assume that that being is as we wish him to be rather than as he is. It is too easy to assimilate the ancient and the different to the present and the self, to read the compensatory imaginings of our own time and our own problems into whatever we regard as authoritative and directive. The most persistent, the most subtle and the most pervasive form of the psychologist's fallacy is that which describes the unseen universe as congruous with our own will, as sharing its nature and contributing to its prosperity and its final happiness. We persist in this, with a sort of dumb, blind faith, even in the face of the ultimate horrors that man may undergo. And this persistence is never so manifest as in most current interpretations of Job. But if Yahweh is somehow human, however remotely and incommensurably, evil becomes, as Job insists, the arbitrary whim of an oriental tyrant, of a bully who, because he is almighty, because he is beyond the reach of retaliation, abuses his strength. That the prologue and epilogue are easily anthropomorphic is of course obvious; but it is no more intelligent to attribute a genuine and vital pathetic fallacy to the author of Job than to Euripides. Both made use of the literary traditions of their races. But for that matter, the dehumanization of God is a conscious and intentional constituent of the Hebraic tradition, and even the orthodoxy of Job's friends attributes *pathos* to divinity only as analogue and overtone. Furthermore, it is hardly thinkable that so profound a writer as the author of our tragedy would make Yahweh acquiesce in a description of himself as an oriental tyrant, however near might be the anthropomorphic infection from the Persian myth of Ormuzd and Ahriman.

If Job is truly an attempt to solve the problem of evil, and inevitably therefore a theory of life, such a description of Yahweh's use of suffering is not a solution of the problem but an aggravation of it. It makes evil more evil. It makes of Job the last word in cynicism. That Job is not intended to be anything of the sort need not be argued, and for this reason alone the usual treatments of the Yahweh of Job must be abandoned. There are however other, as potent, reasons. The whole Hebraic *lebensanschauung* requires it, and the characterizations of deity in the drama itself compels it. The latter seeks in fact to abolish even the analogue and overtone of humanity in God by its refutation of the orthodox belief that evil and suffering are retributive, God having a bias in favor of one way of living as against another, or in favor of one of his creatures as against another. That God should not have a bias was monstrous in the eyes of Job's friends, in the eyes of his nation, in the eyes of all mankind. To the bulk of us it is still monstrous. And it is just this monstrous justice of the cosmic *élan* which is Yahweh that Job asserts of Yahweh, that Yahweh acquiesces in as " the thing that is right " concerning him. In its assertion is attained the ultimate height, the full ripeness of the growth and unfoldment of the Hebraic theory of life. Perforce, it is an impossible step for the mass of mankind to take. The poet's Jewish contemporaries understood it perhaps; it is a view that recurs, much modified and brutalized, in Ecclesiastes, but on the whole Jewish thought stayed with the more comfortable conceptions of the prologue-epilogue, of Eliphaz and his comrades, of Elihu. These still prevail, the world over.

§ 2. *Social Conflicts and Divine Attitudes.*

. . . If, as is the fashion among the advanced theologians of the day, we regard religion as the " consciousness of the highest social values," God, who is the imaginative incarnation and concretion of these values, the one symbol of their manyness, becomes the social soul of which the institutions of society — economic, political, æsthetic and ritual — are the body. As psychologists know, for every change in the body there is a corresponding alteration of soul. The idea of divinity therefore has a history which may be considered as a function of the history of the society that entertains the idea. For obvious reasons, criticism has verified this theory more adequately and minutely upon the idea of divinity entertained by the Jews than upon any other religious idea in history. The upshot is illuminating. Yahweh, it appears, possesses from the very outset a primitive abstractness, an intangibility so unusual to gods of ancient peoples as to be unique. His progress, from the Yahweh of the Kenites who made a covenant with Israel and then grew from Israel's God to the life of the universe, takes place in two simultaneous processes. The first and more outstanding is the process of moralization: the second, much overlaid, but in its dominant phases clear enough, is the process of depersonalization. The two processes culminated by identifying him with the course of nature regarded as a totality, with its energy and dynamic *go*, immanent in all events, transcending each, and making for righteousness.

The primitive Jehovah seems to have stood primarily for those destructive forces in nature which a desert-dwelling, nomadic people learn from their first encounter to fear, to propitiate and to seek alliance with. Philologists declare that the meaning of the root-word of Yahweh might be interpreted indifferently as "to be" or "to destroy," and the early attributes and epithets of Yahweh give color and body to the latter meaning. Although he is without form, hence never to be imaged or represented, his manifestations and attributions are devouring fire, thunder and lightning, pillar of cloud by day and fire by night, desert whirlwind, lord of hosts who leads his chosen in battle, jealous Yahweh and avenging Yahweh. To know him at all, as a rabbinical commentator points out,[1] is to know his *actions*. The loyalty he requires is utter and all-absorbing, and wisdom is the fear of him.

Wisdom remains the fear of him. The wise man was the "God-fearing" man, although the conquest of Canaan, the acquisition of an agricultural economy, the rivalry with other divinities and their absorption by the Israelitish conquest of their worshippers enlarged God's powers and enriched his nature. These changes were inevitable if he was to remain the god of Israel. Extraordinary they were, but nothing else could have happened and the covenant been kept which made Yahweh Israel's God and Israel Yahweh's nation. For the covenant imposed his exclusive worship on Israel, gave him a monopoly of Israel's devotion and service, and how was the god of a nomad organization, the spirit of a culture resting on the possession and care of animals, with its family democracy and economic communism, a spirit having its seat at a desert mountain, to operate in lands beyond his immediate dominion and in an alien economy, resting on tillage, and controlled by the

---

[1] שמי אתה מבקש לידע כפי מעשי אני נקרא "Do you wish to know my name? I am designated by my deeds" (Shevuoth r. c. 3).

chthonic deities who were the soul of that, its patrons
and its guardians? Such operation was impossible.
Yahweh therefore must needs inevitably assimilate the
place and the power of these deities. To his original
attributes of destruction and anger were added theirs
of creation and fertility, and his rôle and worship were
modified accordingly. The change was not consummated without a long struggle. These other divinities
were actively other; they were the divinities of different
and more civilized peoples, rivals of Israel, and their
gods, hence, rivals of Israel's god.

His conquest of them was the achievement of the
Yahwistic party among the tribes of Jacob. At the
outset of the settlement in Canaan that party lived the
life of nomads even in the agricultural state which their
brethren had won. Its members sought to maintain
the nomadic social order in an agricultural economy,
to maintain the democracy and communism of the wan-
dering tribe in a sedentary society. Now it is a universal economic phenomenon that the early equality in
land-holding with which such a society starts is regu-
larly displaced by a spontaneous process of expropria-
tion that culminates in the inequality of a small rich,
land-holding class and a large class of landless and slav-
ery-threatened proletarians. The Yahwistic party
set itself against this process, which is as widespread in
geography as it is recurrent in history, and which is at
the bottom of all the economic problems of modern
states no less than ancient. It opposed nomadic equality to agricultural caste, nomadic communism to agricultural private ownership. The nomadic tradition
which it drew from was a memory turned into an ideal,

a historic social organization of which its divinity was the name and the symbol. The agricultural life which it denounced was a condition, oppugnant to its heart against the nomadic past. The confrontation of the two meant mutual interaccommodation; an interpenetration and confluence whence sprang the new constitution of the state and the new definition of the nature of God. For the nomadic standard in the light of which the agricultural status was denounced, got established in the name of Yahweh as a measure of the fundamental relationships between men and this establishment consisted, in practice, of an identification of Yahweh with righteousness or social justice. Thus the "monotheism" was conserved without being humanized and was rendered "ethical" without being made supernatural.

The prophets were the men responsible for the full elaboration of Yahweh's character as the dynamic of the universe, the life of nature and the judge of men. They and their followers were the party of Yahweh. By their hands the nomadic standard was remolded into agricultural terms, into terms political, and finally into the terms of universal human nature itself.

Historically, this remolding took shape as a warfare between prophet and priest. The latter were the natural opponents of the former. Yahweh, to the prophets, was an elusive, universal potency, overwhelming in its activity, and responsive to conduct only: to the priests he was a specific anthropomorphic power, controllable by ritual.

Thus, consider Amos, the first of the writing prophets. He appears in the reign of Jeroboam II, than whom was none greater among the kings of Israel. What marks his reign, in Amos' judgment, is not the turning of himself and his people to other gods. On the contrary, the priestly organization and ritual at Bethel and other shrines are all that they should be. What marks this great king's reign is rather economic injustice: a commercial class that cheats, a landholding class that revels in luxury and defrauds the poor, a landless class enslaved. Amos directs his bitter denunciations against this whole condition. Now it is to be noted that the Yahweh in whose name Amos speaks is not the old Yahweh of the covenant at Sinai. His nature has expanded from a force chthonic and local into a force cosmic, the moving energy in all reality, maker and destroyer of whatever comes to be or is. Not merely Israel — all nations come under his sway. He is the sole distributor of good and evil, of evil particularly, the avenger of wrongs, and the guarantor of righteousness with prosperity. He is nothing if not retributive, a vindictive Yahweh, that " formeth the mountains and createth the wind, and declareth unto man what is his thought; that maketh the morning darkness and treadeth upon the high places of the earth . . . that maketh the Pleiades and Orion and turneth the shadow of death into morning and maketh the day dark with night; that calleth for the waters of the sea and poureth them out upon the face of earth, that bringeth sudden destruction upon the strong, so that destruction cometh upon the fortress." And the thing he repays is social injustice: the exploitation of the poor by the rich, the betrayal of nation by nation, the ritual "practice" of the church. What he wants is justice and righteousness: "I hate, I despise your feasts, and I will take no delight in your solemn assemblies. Yea, though you do offer me your burnt offerings and meal offerings, I will not accept them; neither will I regard the peace offerings of your fat beasts. Take thou away from me the noise of thy songs, for I will not hear the melody of thy viols. But let justice roll down as the waters, and righteousness as a mighty stream."

Amos sounds the keynote of the class-struggle which dominates the internal history of the Jewish state. His successors only elaborate what he declares, only develop and deepen this condemnation of the alignment he finds so evil; the alignment of king and priest against the people. The champions of Yahweh become concretely the champions of the people, and the menace in Yahweh's name against the shortage of justice and righteousness becomes the menace of masses against classes. Amos' successors extend the rôle and soften the character of Yahweh; they make him tenderer and more pliable, but they all reassert, relevantly to the social setting of their own times, the fundamental propositions of their passionate original. Hosea, Isaiah, Micah, Jeremiah,— the whole mighty line,— urge the same program and speak of Yahweh in the same fashion. Nor are they merely agitators. They are practical statesmen, with independence of vision and clear and distinct ideas of home policy and foreign relations. The Deuteronomic Code is the first formulation of their ideas as law. Jeremiah and his brethren preached it throughout the land, often at the risk of their lives, and it was finally adopted as the formal constitution of the state by the acclamation of all the people.

With the establishment of this code a new phase of the history of the Jewish nation begins. Wherever a written constitution exists life gets standardized, loses mobility, a conflict between the immutable letter and the changing spirit arises. The written law is at one and the same time a guide and a drag. When social and international conditions are inimical to national life and personal happiness, it is a guide; when the very conditions of national life alter at their foundation, as they do in times of prosperity, the written law does not keep pace with the living law, and it becomes a drag. The constitutional history of the United States is the most conspicuous modern instance, and the constitutional history of Judea, with conditions largely reversed, is the most conspicuous ancient instance of both these effects.

Up to the reign of Josiah the Jews considered the unfortunate foreign entanglements of the state as Yahweh's retribution for unrighteousness within. Their struggle against unrighteousness brought them self-consciousness. It led them to themselves, made them aware of their corporate intent; gave the nation possession of its own soul, and they immediately designated this soul or intent as their "mission," as the thing for which they were chosen, for the sake of which they were destined to greatness and prosperity. If righteousness, they thought, was the foundation of prosperity, righteousness was the basis for a world-dominion in which the law was to go forth from Zion and the word of the Lord from Jerusalem. And by means of the second covenant they had set their state upon the rock of righteousness.

But the generation which enacted Deuteronomy into the basic law of the state had not even time to see it through and pass it on to their children. Egyptian imperialistic piracy prevented it from hardening into what it would have had to become if it were to count in fact — the substance of the corporate habit and funded mentality of the race. The principles of Deuteronomy thus did not become a condition — they remained an ideal, a standard for protest rather than a guide for construction. Obedient though he was to the will of God, the good Josiah was killed at Megiddo. Yahweh's failure to keep his part of the covenant provoked a reaction which culminated, as the unhappy and embittered Jeremiah insisted, in the destruction of the Temple and the Babylonian exile.

Of the exiles, the first generation in Babylon exhibit only a formal sense of sin. Sin marks the mood of their children. Their own mood is like despair. Nothing else is uttered by Jeremiah, whose long and tragic life covers the whole period. He had been the most eager for the Deuteronomic reform; he had been, not even excepting Isaiah, its greatest protagonist. He had preached it at the risk of his life. He had undergone the passion of its failure through a brute historic accident, a military plague from Egypt, sent, of course, by Yahweh. He had seen Jerusalem twice taken by Nebuchadnezzar, the temple burned, the walls razed. Why should these misfortunes come if not as retribution for sin? How else could they come, from a just

God! He grew convinced of the horror of sinfulness that tainted his people, citizen and state alike. He urged humble submission to the divine repayment, advocating, in politics and in private life, a policy of non-resistance. The sin was so deep, there was nothing else to do. Barely to live was a grace — to live even the life of an exile. Righteousness was no longer indispensable to prosperity; righteousness was indispensable to mere existence. It is not, he taught, justice that men are any longer to seek; for justice is merely the way to escape from evil. The aim of life must be salvation, salvation, alas, which is the merest salvage of life. For life and death are both in the power of Yahweh and the compulsion of his law must be acquiesced in if the mere good of keeping alive is to be preserved. The status of righteousness has changed from the indispensable minimum for prosperity to the indispensable minimum for self-preservation.

The next generation of the exile, those who had been children when they were sent to Babylon, did not share Jeremiah's resigned despair. They had drunk the waters of Babylon even while they wept by them. For them, Deuteronomy, which their fathers and grandfathers had cast off as a practice, became precious as an ideal. Memory set standards to which this generation assimilated and by means of which it recreated much of the hieratic system and much of the mythology of the conqueror, Hebraizing them throughout. They were simply added to the old fervor and the old vision, not substituted for them; the passionate humanism, the ethical inwardness, the devotion to righteousness remained at the core. Even Ezekiel, priest-minded

though he is, expresses it, and its great witness is the
Levitical Code. The hope also of imperial dominion
remained.

But all these are chastened, sobered, spiritualized.
The Jews of the exile realized as no other nation did
the horrors of war and the immoralities of empire.
For war the prophets offered peace; for empire, international comity. A program of international peace, of
universal peace, of peace as a positive ideal, and of a
democratic internationalism which only a theocracy
could be in those days, appears for the first time in history as a governing program of a group of men deeply
concerned with the realities of living. The God who
was to realize these ideals had to be correspondingly
greater, subtler, more impersonal. *All* the courses of
events had to be expressions of his intent, for if any
were not, his omnipotence, and hence the guarantee of
ultimate prosperity for Israel which that omnipotence
was, would be impaired. Yahweh consequently becomes the cosmic force itself, the stream of creative
activity, moving as universal history; source of both
good and evil; to whom things and empires are tools
taken up and cast aside; who has no like, a being in-
commensurate with all things thinkable, but who none
the less makes for righteousness and can do no wrong.
The more apparently hopeless the situation of the Jewish people, the more widespread their exile, and the
darker their prospect, the more powerful must be their
God, the more unhuman the activity which should restore and realize their hope, gather up their scattered
remnants, and transfigure their outlook. From such
a social mood grows the Yahweh who inspires the

oracles and prophecies of the unknown writer called deutero-Isaiah: the might and majesty of God waxed with the weakness and meanness of his nation that needed his salvation.

§ 3. *The " Suffering Servant " and the Joban Indictment of God.*

With this universalization of Yahweh into the transcendental dynamic of all reality came also, however, a change of mood.

Yahweh of Hosts is omnipotent; he can save but does not. Why? Surely his promises are to be fulfilled, surely Israel has suffered enough and is to be restored! Yes, the seed of Jacob *is* restored, but even restored, suffers on. What then can be the meaning of this suffering?

By a psychological process original to the nature of man, a process, best designated by the word " compensation " and as observable in groups as in individuals, there takes shape, as response to disadvantage, an interpretation of the disadvantage favorable to its victim. If God causes his chosen people to suffer, this interpretation declares, then the suffering and the choice are co-implicative: indeed, suffering *is* choice. So a defect, considered constitutional, intrinsic, is converted into a virtue. Such compensatory conversion is what, for example, distinguishes the contemporary reformed sects among the Jews: in the prophetic tradition it was, however, only a passing phase. When it arose, it served to throw the whole history of Jewry into a perspective which showed each disaster as one in a series of lustrations whereby the chosen people were being purged, lustrations destined to culminate in the restoration of the Jewish state, in the Golden Age when all the nations were to worship Yahweh alone and cleave to the Jew because of his nearness to Yahweh. The reformed sects in modern Jewry have dropped the essentially prophetic ideal of restoration. What the latter regarded as exile and what the latter regarded as mission are one for the former. According to reformed theology, Israel is scattered among the nations and suffers among them, because he is designated as a light unto the Gentiles, and so alone can he illumine the Gentile darkness. Such a doctrine is, of course, diametrically opposed to the prophetic hope and the prophetic policy and the prophetic political and religious realism. That saw a golden age in which all the exiles were to return and a just state to be established in truth and in peace. Then, the prophet Zechariah writes, "Many people and strong nations shall come to seek Yahweh of Hosts in Jerusalem, and to entreat the favor of Yahweh. . . . Ten men shall take hold, out of all the languages of the nations, they shall take hold of the skirts of him that is a Jew, saying we will go with you, for we have heard that God is with you."

Zechariah's millennial vision is one of the markings of the second phase of the prophetic theory of life. It was not without its raison d'être in the political conditions of his time. The handful of patriotic Utopians who had availed themselves of Cyrus' permission to return to Palestine and rebuild the Temple found a denuded land, a degraded peasantry and hostile neighbors. Taxes were intolerably heavy and it is not im-

probable that without the support of magnates and
idealists whose interest or inclination kept them in
exile the enterprise would have gone to pieces for lack
of means alone. But there were other difficulties, more
serious. The Samaritans, descendants of settlers
placed by Shalmanessar IV in the lands from which he
had exiled the ten tribes, had at first made overtures
of cooperation to the Jews, and had been rejected.
The rejection converted them into relentless and un-
forgetting enemies. They began and successfully executed intrigues to prevent the rebuilding of the temple,
their influence inducing the Persian authorities to for-
bid operations. Sixteen years passed before these were
resumed.

The whole of this period in Palestine is very largely
a blank to us. Zerubbabel, son of Shealtiel, of Davidic
stock, governor of Judah, and Joshua, son of Josedek
the high priest, who together led the community, seem
to have succeeded only in marking time. That misfortune had not destroyed the political instinct nor
dimmed the political hope, that Jews both within and
without Palestine dreamed of independence and worked
for it, waiting only favorable conditions to act, subsequent events showed. The favorable conditions
came, they thought, with the death of Cyrus, which
threw the empire he had won with the sword and kept
with kindliness under the shock of usurpation and rebellion. Cambyses, Smerdis, Darius succeeded one another in short order, and the last was elevated to the
throne only to be confronted by uprisings in every
quarter of his empire except the west. To the prophets of the period in Judah, Haggai and Zechariah, the

time seemed favorable for the renewal of national activity, the rebuilding of the temple and the formal establishment of the state. The power of the enemies and persecutors of Judah, they prophesy, is to be shattered: the Messiah, Zerubbabel, son of David, is to be acknowledged, and the Golden Age to begin.

"And the word of Yahweh came," writes Haggai, . . . "speak to Zerubbabel, governor of Judah, saying, I will shake the heavens and the earth, and I will overthrow the throne of kingdoms, and I will destroy the strength of the kingdoms of the nations, and I will overthrow the chariots and those that ride in them and the horses and their riders shall come down, every one by the sword of his brother. In that day, saith Yahweh of Hosts will I take thee, O Zerubbabel, my servant, the son of Shealtiel, saith Yahweh, and I will make thee as a signet. For I have chosen thee saith Yahweh of Hosts." Zechariah is even more fervid in his promises for the future to Zerubbabel, whom he conspicuously entitles Branch, Servant of God. He is to rebuild the temple, to renew the state and to bring the people prosperity.

To him the description of Isaiah XLII 1–9 applies in like tenor: "Behold my servant, whom I uphold; my chosen, in whom my soul delighteth. I have put my spirit upon him; he will bring forth justice to the Gentiles. He will not cry, nor lift up his voice, nor cause it to be heard in the street. A bruised reed will he not break, and a dimly-burning wick will he not quench: he will bring forth justice in truth. He will not fail nor be discouraged till he have set justice in the earth, and the isles shall wait for his law.

"Thus saith God Yahweh, he that created the heavens and stretched them forth, he that spread abroad the earth and that which cometh out of it, he that giveth breath unto the people upon it and unto them that walk therein: 'I, Yahweh, have called thee in righteousness and will hold thy hand and will keep thee and give thee for a covenant of the people, for a light of the Gentiles, to open the blind eyes, to bring out the prisoners from the dungeons, and them that sit in darkness out of the prison house. I am Yahweh: that is my name, and my glory will I not give to another, neither my praise unto graven images. Behold the former things are come to pass, and new things do I declare: before they spring forth I tell you of them.' " Zerubbabel is to be the liberator and vindicator of his people. The event is imminent although secret. But Isaiah XLIX [1] 1–13 is even more explicit. The chosen servant of Yahweh is to raise up the tribes of Jacob; a mere servant of rulers, he is to become the master of kings, to liberate Israel, to bring them prosperity. Through him the very world is to find salvation. "Sing, O heavens! and be joyful, O earth! Break forth into singing, O mountains: for Yahweh hath comforted his people and will have compassion upon his afflicted!" This was to come about, declared Zechariah, "not by might, and not by strength," but by the spirit of the Lord. Zerubbabel has been destined by Yahweh to be his servant, to re-establish Israel, to in-

[1] The identification of the "Servant of the Lord" in Isaiah with Zerubbabel was first made and defended at considerable length by Sellin, who afterward retracted a number of his propositions.

itiate the Golden Age. "Behold," writes the unknown author of Isaiah LII 13–15, "behold, my servant shall deal wisely, he shall be exalted and lifted up and shall be very high. Like as many were astonished at thee (his visage was so marred more than any man, and his form more than the sons of men) so shall he startle many nations: kings shall shut their mouths at him; for that which has not been told them shall they see, and that which they had not heard shall they understand."

The prophetic incitement to the rebuilding of the Temple, the oracles of the restoration of national independence (the latter, as the citations perhaps show, only symbolized by the prophets, or at most hinted at rather than explicitly declared, for it was a dangerous thing to talk about, much more to undertake), bore fruit in action. Building was begun anew. Patriots from Babylon sent representatives to Palestine with a crown of gold and silver that Zechariah crowned Zerubbabel with. The undertaking was secretly planned and secretly executed. The Babylonian patriots took the crown home with them, and the record ends. (Zechariah VI, 9–15.)

Persia's history as well as Judah's own testifies that the hopes of national independence and of the assumption of David's crown by the Scion of David were unrealized. Darius crushed his enemies and consolidated his dominions even more strongly than Cyrus. Zerubbabel disappears from the scene. But, curiously, the rebuilding of the temple is completed by the elders of Israel, and under a decree of Darius. The authority for this is Ezra. Zerubbabel is not mentioned among the elders, but the prophesying of Haggai and

Zechariah both are. The house was finished, Ezra writes, " on the third day of the month Adar, which was in the sixth year of the reign of Darius the king."

Zerubbabel passes from history between the second and the sixth year of Darius' reign. His absence from Ezra's record and the silence of the prophets concerning him are significantly conspicuous. Prince and Branch of the House of David, Servant of God, Messiah, symbol of the hope of Judah, how could his death have passed unmentioned if it had been natural, if it had not become jeopardy to name him, treachery to Persian power even to speak of him? The completion of the temple with the permission and encouragement of Darius and the ominous omission of the very name of Zerubbabel, of mention even of his death by a writer like Ezra are no mere coincidence. They suggest that the secret crowning of Zerubbabel was discovered or betrayed, probably betrayed, that Zerubbabel took all the blame and paid the price, that in a word, Zerubbabel is the suffering servant, the announced liberator who was to enfranchise the slaves, rebuild the state, install the Golden Age, and who instead became the voluntary scapegoat of the patriots. Of whom could the prophet cry with more justice, as he cries, in Isaiah LIII: " Who hath believed our message, and to whom hath the arm of Yahweh been revealed? For he grew up before him as a tender plant, and as a root out of the dry ground. He hath no form nor comeliness, and when we see him there is no beauty that we should desire him. He was despised and rejected of men, a man of sorrows and acquainted with grief, and as one from whom men hide their face despised. And we esteemed him not.

"Surely he hath borne our griefs and carried our sorrows, yet we did esteem him stricken, smitten of God and afflicted. But he was wounded for our transgressions, he was bruised for our iniquities; the chastisement of our peace was upon him, and with his stripes we are healed. All we like sheep have gone astray: we have turned every one to his own way, and Yahweh hath laid upon him the iniquity of us all.

"He was oppressed, yet when he was afflicted he opened not his mouth. As a lamb that is led to the slaughter, and as a sheep that before its shearers is dumb, so he opened not his mouth. By oppression and judgment he was taken away, and as for his generation, who among them considered that he was cut off out of the land of the living for the transgression of my people to whom the stroke was due? And they made his grave with the wicked, and with a rich man in his death, although he had done no violence, neither was any deceit in is mouth.

"Yet it pleased Yahweh to bruise him. He hath put him to grief. . . . For he poured out his soul unto death and was numbered with the transgressors: yet he bare the sin of many and made intercession for the transgressors."

If this applies to Zerubbabel, and so far as our knowledge goes there is hardly any other historic person of the period to whom it can so appropriately apply, the problem of Job must have gotten in his fate its first highly notable concrete and dramatic incarnation, an incarnation which would have brought it home at intensest poignancy to all thoughtful Jews, and have kept it before their minds for generations to come. The events of the ensuing period, enough in themselves perhaps to raise the problem, would have aggravated it if it were already present to their consciousness.

For the Davidic stock seems to have given out, and with it, the hope of national independence. That is replaced by concentration on the church as an institution, and the church in its turn becomes the occasion for the rise of a hieratic bureaucracy which exploited and taxed the *Am Ha'arez* in God's name. Nehemiah's narrative discloses an astounding departure from fundamental law, a departure which he corrects but fails to abolish. The Jews he speaks of are a subject people, absorbed in temple and ritual; impoverished through taxation and defenceless through injustice; surrounded by malevolent and intriguing enemies whose one aim was to keep them weak. Hopeless of any living autonomy, they yielded to the tendency of all hopelessness, the tendency to withdraw from the world of real contacts, to compensate for the world of fact with a world of fancy, to adopt for the spirit an otherworldly habitation, to enchannel the energies that would otherwise have been absorbed by the life of reason in the sedulous and precise practice of ritual, to identify righteousness with this practice, to become, in short, a church, with a religion of disillusion. The Greeks, on their first encounters with Palestinian Jews, were inclined to regard them as a sect of philosophers, and so far as the prophetic insight governed the latter, not altogether wrongly.

But the prophetic insight was changing from a program to be carried out into a dogma to be merely asserted. The prophets passed when the high priest became the prince also. A church-state has no room for the spontaneous religiousness and protestant spirit of prophecy. Its place gets taken by the less passionate " wisdom," and the practical prophet gives way to the reflective wise man. The latter is heir not only to the prophet's place, but to his struggle with the priests. Job represents the unique surviving recorded phase of that struggle before the beginning of the Hellenistic era.

In Job, the prophetic ideals are still vital and prophetic conceptions still dominant. For the period to which it belongs righteousness is yet far from ritual. God still enforces good conduct, rewarding merit and punishing iniquity; Nehemiah calls divine attention repeatedly to his own just deeds, and as repeatedly to wickedness in the enemies of Judah. In point of fact the Jews were so beset by foes and so powerless against them that the ideal of divine retribution defined itself in terms of compensation such that a wished-for future would redress the evil balance of the unpleasant present. Almost every one of the prophetic writings contains plentiful insertions of oracles concerning the hard fate of the persecutors of Israel: the Jews were peacefully taking out in vituperation what they knew was impossible to accomplish in fact. Conversely, as their enemy's present advantage was to be redressed by future misfortune, so their own degradation now was to be balanced by the high honors of a later time.

§ 4. *The Nature of God.*

But all such readjustment required change, and to the Jews consequently the idea of change, of becoming, of futurity, was both empirically and metaphysically real: the Golden Age was something to come, an event anticipated, and different from and better than the present. The power that could bring this event to be, had, hence, of itself to be a real energy, dynamic, creative, a force manifesting itself in the *history* far more than in the structure of the world. The difference between this force and its manifestations is nowhere explicitly indicated. God is immanent in the movement of events: each is an aspect of him, each reveals him, yet he transcends each and all as such. He is, to the prophets, nothing anthropomorphic — the dynamic unity, or better, the dynamic continuity of nature, the creative history of the universe, that is only occasionally a shaping Providence, but always an all-generating and all-destroying Power. Even his making for righteousness is natural, here. For in the business of living, from day to day, good and evil actions meet their due in the course of events; conduct and destiny are correlated as cause and effect; there is nothing intervening, nothing judicial, personal, voluntary: the regulation of conduct is continuous, automatic, and natural. As overeating is correlative with indigestion, indolence with poverty, so are wickedness with disaster and righteousness with well-being. God is the something not ourselves that makes for righteousness, indeed, and what was important to the priestly bureaucracy and to the hopes and fears of the people was that it *should* make for righteousness. This was the heart of orthodoxy.

But when Job appears righteousness is already on the way to ritual; dogmas are hardening and religious practices are getting standardized; religion is becoming specifically differentiated from life, and the church motive is very nearly the sole controlling motive. The real ruler of Judah is the High Priest. He administers the law and frees from sin. It is under his dominion and with reference to the priestly caste and its dependents that the tradition of Judaism, as a distinct strain within the Hebraic tradition, gets established and its modifications of the original Hebraic documents, which we call the Holy Bible, conserved. The aim of the redactions of these is, of course, to keep the ruling class easily in power, to preserve and enlarge their interest, vested in keeping state secondary to and dependent upon church. The redactions of the historical material, of the books of the prophets, of even the wisdom books are made to harmonize with the officially acceptable theory concerning the wishes of God, the duties of man and the privileges of priests, and this is retributive in its fundamental. That there must have been any number of dissenting writers the mere existence of the book of Job witnesses, and that they should have failed to get preserved their dissent would make natural, indeed, inevitable, to any one familiar with the methods of churches and the fate of heretics. Job's preservation is clearly due to its apparent conformity to the official doctrine. This probably saved it from the holocaust which was the lot of the prophecies of Jeremiah. The author of Job, like Euripides, knew the wisdom of conveying his heterodox doctrine by means of a seductive orthodox setting, and of so putting the seal of ultimate approval on the heterodoxy.

But with all its divergences from orthodoxy, Job is not a break with the Hebraic tradition. Rather is it a courageous continuation of that tradition, its most profound, its most vital and logical culmination. It is the summing up and generalization of the historic experience of the Jewish people. The God of Job is like the God of the prophets — the force of nature, manifesting itself with greatest clearness and definiteness in the movement of the universe rather than in its structure. The terms in which he is described throughout the drama are terms of action: the usual hypostasis of the pleasant emotions of men, of love, of goodness, of charity, is not made. The only human attribute declared of God is the attribute of justice and that gets a peculiar significance through the fact that it is treated as an implication of his omnipotence. God is the dynamic of the universe, and the range of his power is coextensive with it. His omnipotence is not deduced dialectically, it is observed empirically: Yahweh is the creator of heaven and earth, the *élan* of the whole panorama of nature, the source of both good and evil, the adjuster of destiny for men. In human terms he cannot be thought; being omnipotent, he is self-sufficient, absolute, consequently altogether incommensurable with human nature, the irreduceable surd of all experience, whose being and force can be acknowledged, but not reasoned with. There is no common measure,

WORD OF THE WEEK

The Subject: God ordains certain men to hell on purpose

Isaiah 84:8 - O Lord, thou art our Father; we are the clay; and thou our potter; and we all are the work of thy hand.

> work - Hebrew: Maaseh-an action (good or bad); product; transaction; business

Romans 9:20-23 - Who art thou that repliest against God? Shall the thing formed say to him that formed it, why hast thou made me thus? Hath not the potter the power over the clay of the same lump, to make one vessel unto honour and another unto dishonour -- What if God willing to show his wrath, and to make his power known, endured with much long suffering the vessels of wrath fitted to destruction: And that he might make known the riches of his glory on the vessels of mercy, which he hath afore prepared unto glory.

> fitted - Greek: katartizo - to complete thoroughly; fit; frame; arrange; prepare. Thayer says this word speaks of men whose souls God has so constituted that they cannot escape destruction; their mind is fixed that they frame themselves.

Men get angry to think that we serve a God that can do as it pleases him. They actually think that an almighty God thinks the way they think and that he could not possibly form-fit a vessel to hell merely to show his wrath and power. Paul said he does. Men have difficulty perceiving a God that predestinates men (Rom. 8:29) on whom he desires to show his grace (unmerited favor) and mercy, that he may shower them throughout eternity with the riches of his glory. We like to believe that we must give him permission; if he is to operate in our hearts and minds. The Lord said, "My thoughts are not your thoughts, neither are your ways my ways. As the heavens are higher than the earth, so are my ways higher than your ways and my thoughts than your thoughts (Isaiah 55:8,9)". Our God is in the heavens: he hath done whatsoever he hath pleased (Psalms 115:3). He doeth whatsoever pleaseth him (Eccl 8:3). Thou, O Lord hast done as it pleased thee (Jonah 1:14). Whatsoever the Lord pleased, that did he in heaven, and earth, and in the seas, and in all deep places (Psalms 135:6). He does all his pleasure (Isa. 46:10; Isa. 44:24-28; Eph. 1:5,9; Philippians 2:13). It is Jesus that holds the keys to death and hell (Rev. 1:18), not Satan. God will intentionally cast these evil vessels of wrath into hell and lock them up for eternity because it is not his pleasure to draw them to him (John 6:44). This doctrine angers men, though it is taught throughout the pages of God's Holy Book. Men do not have a Biblical view of the living God when they think he is not in control of all things including the minds and hearts of all men. God is not only love to the vessels of mercy, but he is a consuming fire (Deut 4:24) upon the vessels of wrath fitted to destruction. We do not serve a God who is Superman that can only shake mountains, implode blackholes, and explode quasars. The God of the universe can harden and soften the hearts of men at will (Rom 9:18; Ezek. 36:26). He giveth not account of any of his matters (Job 33:13).

GRACE AND TRUTH MINISTRIES
P.O. Box 1109 Hendersonville, TN 37077
Jim Brown - Bible Teacher • 824-8502

Radio Broadcast – Sat. Morn. 8am 1300 AM Dial WNQM
TV – Mon. & Sat 10pm, Wed. & Fri. 12am Channel 176;
Tues. & Thurs. 5pm Channel 3; Thurs. 11am Channel 49

Join us for fellowship at 394 West Main Street on
Sunday Mornings @ 11:00am, Sunday Evenings @ 7:00pm,
Wednesday Evenings @ 7:00pm
Or
Watch us live via U-Stream on the web at
www.graceandtruth.net

no *ratio,* between the infinite energy which is the life
of the world and its creature, man, with all his interests and bias.

Both Job and his comforters are agreed on this:
they vie with each other in the completeness of their
pronouncements concerning it. But the consequences
they draw from it are contradictory. Because there
is no common measure, declare Eliphaz and his comrades, there can be for God no standards, no responsibility, no morality. These derive from God and are
binding upon men. But since they derive from God,
how can they be binding upon God? That any man
should ask God " to enter into judgment with man "
is, hence, presumption, blasphemy. Job, on the contrary, holds that God's responsibility to himself alone
is irresponsibility. And Yahweh concurs in this conception of his status: " Who then is he," he asks of
Job, " who can stand before me? Who hath given
unto me, that I should repay him? Whatsoever is
over the whole heaven is mine." There can be no common denominator between God and man, and every attempt to establish one proves abortive.

Indeed, every demonstration of a particular moral
direction in the universe can be met by an equally
cogent demonstration of a will or *élan* in the opposite
direction. At worst God is unmoral, just with the
justice of indifference. At best he is inscrutable,
opaque, a self-revelation unrevealing of anything at all.
" Canst thou by searching find out God? Canst thou
find out the almighty unto perfection? It is as high as
heaven: what canst thou do? Deeper than sheol; what
canst thou know? The measure thereof is larger than

the earth and broader than the sea," Zophar declares to Job, reaffirming the universal compulsion, the inescapable grip of the principle underlying Job's earlier complaint:

> " Lo, he goeth by me, and I see him not.
> He passeth on, also, and I perceive him not.
> Lo, he springs on the prey: who can hinder him?
> Who will say unto him, What doest thou? "

The divine suddenness and divine elusiveness are one and the same.

> " Behold, I go forward, and he is not there,
> And backward, but I cannot perceive him;
> On the left hand, where he doth work, but I cannot behold
>   him:
> He hideth himself on the right hand, that I cannot see him."

It is for this reason that the author of Job insists on our taking at its face value that revelation of Yahweh in nature and in society which is our experience; on our accepting as coordinate the lovingkindness and providence of the Lord with his cruelty and immorality. God's standards are not man's standards, nor God's ways man's ways: in the essential, the wicked also prosper, also the righteous go down to defeat. From any point of view that is human that you may choose, God has no preferences nor can his will and interests be defined in terms of preference. He is the dynamical life of *all* nature, and he needs must be just to all. But this justice is nothing like the justice man conceives of and desires. Retribution it certainly is not. What is it then? Under the most favorable and deepest construction it is the recognition that the life which is the source and foundation of all lives, pertains to them all impartially, that it favors none of its creatures more than any other. Yahweh describes himself as the wisdom which makes for the survival of the wild ass, the hawk, the eagle, the ostrich, of all living nature, and the wisdom that uproots mountains and annihilates angels. His justice is his wisdom, and this again is nothing else than power, force, the go and potency, generative and disintegrative, in things. It possesses nothing of the moral or the human; it is not foresight but performance, the originative and annihilative flowing of nature. His wisdom and might, his counsel and understanding are: to break up past rebuilding, to shut up past opening, to dry up the waters and to send them out so that they overturn the earth.

With him is strength and wisdom;
The deceived and the deceiver are his.
He leadeth counsellors away stripped,
And judges maketh he fools.
He looseth the bond of kings,
And bindeth their loins with a girdle.
He leadeth priests away stripped,
And overthroweth the mighty.
He removeth the speech of the trusty,
And taketh away the understanding of the elders.
He poureth contempt upon princes,
And looseth the belt of the strong.
He uncovereth deep things out of darkness,
And bringeth out to light the shadow of death.
He increaseth the nations, and he destroyeth them:

He enlargeth the nations, and he leadeth them captive.
He taketh away understanding from the chiefs of the
  people of the earth,
And causeth them to wander in the wilderness where there
  is no way.
They grope in the dark without light;
And he maketh them to stagger like a drunken man.

According to the private bias of the human spirit, according to the preferences of man, considering the need
of man alone, out of the very core of human nature,
God is unjust and cannot and should not be justified.
"God hath subverted me in my cause," cries Job,

I cry out of wrong, but I am not heard,
I cry for help, but there is no justice.

For the divine action beats on indifferently, or if you
prefer, with equal care, for each and all of its creations. Its providence is in the fall of a sparrow, and
microbe and man are alike its concern. Description
and definition of it, please note, invariably proceeds by
means of dynamic terms. It is a narrative of things
doing, a history, not the analysis of a purpose nor
the designation of a reason. God is Action, not
Thought, and his reality is Change. Hebrew, significantly, possesses no word for *eternity:* The nearest
approach to it are " everlasting," " enduring," " world
without end," literally, " world, and beyond." God is
Temporality, Becoming, and it is essentially as temporality, as the force that alters and creates, that he
constitutes the ultimate environment of the human
spirit. To it, morally indifferent, the spirit of man

must adapt itself, must know it, propitiate it, control it. His relations with it are of ultimate importance to him; indifferent to it. What he does can concern only his own realization of his inner worth and destiny, not God. All the protagonists of the tragedy — Job, Eliphaz and his comrades, Elihu, assert this fact. It is another common ground for their divergent conclusions.

§ 5. *The Excellence Proper to Man; The Destiny of Man.*

What then, is man, and what is his status with regard to this all-enveloping and overwhelming changeful force in which he lives and moves and has his being? This force, clearly, did not come to be with him in view, nor had it especial regard for him in any of its creations. The world he lives in is not one which was made for him, but one in which he grew, and one in which he can maintain himself only by eternal vigilance: it is the *fear* of the Lord that is the beginning of wisdom. Man, says the poet, is born unto trouble, as the sparks fly upward. There is a warfare to him upon earth; he is born upon it, he dwells on it only by the mercy of the surrounding omnipotence, and then he dies. With death his hapless story ends. A more acceptable fate may be hoped for, but never achieved.

Man that is born of woman,
Is of few days, and full of trouble.
He cometh forth like a flower, and is cut down:
He fleeth also as a shadow, and continueth not.
And dost thou open thine eyes upon such an one,

And bringest me into judgment with thee?
Who can bring a clean thing out of an unclean? not one.
Seeing his days are determined
The number of his months is with thee,
And thou hast appointed his bounds that he cannot pass;
Look away from him, that he may rest,
Till he shall accomplish, as a hireling, his day.
For there is hope of a tree,
If it be cut down, that it will sprout again,
And that the tender branch thereof will not cease.
Though the root thereof wax old in the earth,
And the stock thereof die in the ground;
Yet through the scent of water it will bud,
And put forth boughs like a plant.
But man dieth, and is laid low:
Yea, man giveth up the ghost, and where is he?
As the waters fail from the sea,
And the river wasteth and drieth up;
So man lieth down and riseth not:
Till the heavens be no more, they shall not awake,
Nor be roused out of their sleep.
Oh that thou wouldest hide me in Sheol!
That thou wouldest keep me secret, until thy wrath be past,
That thou wouldest appoint me a set time, and remember
  me!
. . . If a man die, shall he live again? —
All the days of my warfare would I wait,
Till my release should come.
Thou wouldest call, and I would answer thee:
Thou wouldest have a desire to the work of thy hands.

  .   .   .   .

But the mountain, falling, cometh to nought;
And the rock is removed out of its place;
The waters wear away the stones;
The overflowings thereof wash away the dust of the earth:

So thou destroyest the hope of man.
Thou prevailest forever against him, and he passeth;
Thou changest his countenance, and sendest him away.

Merely to live as he lives, man needs the fear of the
Lord — needs that wisdom which is to be gathered by
the observation of nature, the study of history, the
companionship of the wise. This is a wisdom which has
nothing of the theoretical. Pure reason is its opposite.
Its essence rather is practical intelligence, gumption,
the knowledge of what to do, and how to do it in the
face of inharmonious situations and the march of time.
It is foresight rather than insight, or better, it is the
identification of insight with foresight. It is a thing
empirical and reasonable, rather than logical and ra-
tional. It assumes the reality of Change and Time,
and its vision is a vision of adjustment rather than a
vision of existence. As the refrain of the first chorus
declares it:

The fear of the Lord is the beginning of Wisdom,
And to depart from evil, understanding.

And what does this painfully-conditioned wisdom of
man teach him concerning himself? It teaches him
first of all its own weakness. Even as the righteousness which is the departure from evil, even as the vigilance which is the fear of the Lord, it fails to be a guarantee for prosperity: the viable and labile Cosmic
Energy may be redirected by it; but also it may not.
Suffering and death do not consider whether a man
has been of the righteous or of the wicked. "They
lie down alike in the dust, and the worm covereth

them." God, being indeed transcendental, transcends morality and manlike justice as well as everything else. For the justice which is his attribute, I cannot repeat too often, is just that justice of indifference, of cosmic impartiality whereby each creature of God's might makes its own destiny according to the implications of its own nature, without hindrance and without help. If, therefore, man seeks righteousness, he seeks it not because of any extrinsic advantage, but because being what he is, righteousness is his proper virtue, the security and fulfillment of his inward excellence. If the righteous man falls, the Divine Will becomes in the fall the vindicator and avenger of the victim against its very self, for in the irrevocable and unalterable past there remains, irrevocably passed, the tragic event. But a vindication of the dead does the dead no good. A future life might make the situation endurable; death is, however, complete extinction.

Consequently the ultimate value of human existence is not existence merely; the ultimate value of human existence is the quality and distinction of existence of which consists a man's character, his nature as this or that kind of man. "Behold," declares Job, "I know that he will slay me; I have no hope. Nevertheless will I maintain my ways before him." "Till I die will I not put away mine integrity from me; my righteousness hold I fast, and will not let it go. My heart shall not reproach me so long as I live."

To cling to his integrity while he lives, to assert and to realize the excellences appropriate to his nature as a man, as this particular kind of man, knowing all the while that this is to be accomplished in a world which

was not made for him, in which he shares his claim
on the consideration of Omnipotence with the infinitude
of its creatures that alike manifest its powers — this is
the destiny of man. He must take his chance in a world
that doesn't care about him any more than about anything else. He must maintain his ways with courage
rather than with faith, with self-respect rather than
with humility or better perhaps, with a faith that is
courage, a humility that is self-respect. When ulti-
mately confronted with the inward character of Omnipotence, man realizes that, on its part, alone moral
indifference can be genuine justice. Its providence, its
indifference, its justice — they are all one. Otherwise nothing else but the favored, the chosen creature
could exist. Hence, when Yahweh reveals himself to
Job as the creative providence sustaining even the most
impotent of living things and destroying even the
strongest, Job realizes that not prosperity but excellence is the justification of human life, and the very
indifference of Yahweh comforts him. " I know " he
declares,

that thou canst do all things,
And that no purpose of thine can be restrained.
By hearsay only had I heard of thee,
But now mine eyes seeth thee,
Wherefore I recant my challenge, and am comforted
Amid dust and ashes.

§ 6. Conclusion: The Humanism of the Hebraic Mind.

Such is the theory of life in which the ripest wisdom

of the Hebraic tradition found expression. Its beginnings are strong in Jeremiah, its growth is a function of the progressive postponement of Yahweh's promised Golden Age, of the irony of a chosen people that suffers, of individual tragedies like Jeremiah's and Zerubbabel's. In it the soul of man comes to itself and is freed. It is a humanism terrible and unique. For unlike the Greek humanism it does not enfranchise the mind by interpreting the world in terms of its own substance, by declaring an ultimate happy destiny for man in a world immortally in harmony with his nature and needs; it is not an anthropomorphosis, not a pathetic fallacy. It is without illusion concerning the quality, extent and possibilities of the life of man, without illusion concerning his relation to God. It accepts them, and makes of the human soul the citadel of man — even against Omnipotence itself — wherein he cherishes his integrity, and so cherishing, is victorious in the warfare of living even when life is lost.

This is why, on the confrontation of Hebraism with Hellenism, Hellenism conquered the Jewish mind itself: why the philosophic tradition has been dominated by Greek ideas, why religion has remained illusion rather than vision, why it is only with the coming of science that Hebraism begins to come into its own. For science yields power where it creates disillusion; it is a conquest of nature through knowledge. But the Hebraic mind had in Job attained disillusion without such compensating mastery of nature: its science was childishness. It had attained disillusion only with mastery of self, and such an excellence is too rare and difficult ever to become a common virtue of mankind.

PART III

THE PRESENT TEXT OF THE BOOK OF JOB

III

The text used for the present edition of the book of Job is that of the American Revised Version. Very few departures from it have been made, and those made were compelled by the necessities of accuracy, accuracy being indispensable to dramatic propriety. The outstanding change comes in Job's last speech, XLII, 6. The ordinary reading is:

> . . . I abhor myself
> And repent in dust and ashes.

For this I have written

> I recant my challenge, and am comforted
> Amid dust and ashes.

Concerning the meaning of *nikhamti,* which the regular versions translate " repent," there cannot, I think, be much question. Its root means " comfort," and the whole purport of the drama holds the word to this meaning: Job's friends come to comfort him and fail; God comes, answering Job's challenge, and succeeds. This leads Job to withdraw the challenge. The traditional rendering is false as it stands, as the idiomatic use of *nikhamti* with *ăl,* which is translatable as " repent," would require Job to repent or be sorry about, not *in,* dust and ashes. Such guidance as the meter here offers allows many other alternatives and the movement of the dialogue alone can help to decide which is most fitting. Concerning *emas,* the question is less closed. But " recant " seems to me to be closer to the dramatic situation and the context as a whole. Besides, it has the high authority of Nathaniel Schmidt. Other changes have involved merely the grammatical proprieties of the English language.

Save the *Shemà:* Shemà, Yisrael, Yahweh Elohenu Yahweh Ehad, nothing has been added to the text. Job's remarks I, 21, " The Lord gave, and the Lord hath taken away, blessed be the name of the Lord," have been put also in the mouth of the chorus, and other transpositions and rearrangements occur throughout the play. Only the former is arbitrary. The others are demanded by the character of the text itself and are made on authority. Thus Chapters XXVIII; XXIV 2–24; XL, 15–24; XLI, have been assigned to the Chorus. Verses 26 and 27, of Chapter XIX have been omitted, as an obvious interpolation, contradicting both the spirit and the letter of the rest of the chapter. Verse 16, Chapter XXI belongs evidently to Eliphaz: it can be nothing else than a reply to Job, verse 17 having the character of a retort on Job's part. Similarly, verse 19 in the same chapter goes to Bildad, and is indeed, in keeping with his character, as is verse 22 with Zophar's, to whom it has been assigned. Verse 18 Chapter XXII, is absurd except in the mouth of Job, while verses 1 to 6, Chapter XXVI to verse 7, Chapter XXVII, cannot belong to anyone else. Verses 5 to 14, of the previous chapter, 13 to 23 of Chapter XXVII are evidently continuous with Bildad's too short speech of Chapter XXV, while verses 7 to 23 of Chapter XXVII and verse 25 of Chapter XXIV would naturally go to Zophar, with whose character they are in keeping. Verses 1, 11, 12 of Chapter XXXI have been omitted, and the rest of the text has been rearranged in climactic order.

Elihu's speech has been slightly condensed at points, and

has been broken up. The omissions are verses 8, 9, 10, 13, 14, 18, 21 to the end of Chapter XXXII; 2, 3, 4 and 33 of XXXIII; 4 of XXXVI. Verses 5 to 16 of Chapter 36 and verses 26 to 30 of the same chapter have been assigned to members of the chorus. Elihu speaks the rest.

From the speech of Yahweh, verses 10 and 11 of Chapter XLI have been transposed to where they seem to belong — right after Job's speech, XLII, 2, and this comes most appropriately just after Yahweh has finished the recital of his powers, namely after XL, 2, where it has accordingly been set. Finally the first half of verse 3 and the whole of verse 4, of the same chapter, have been omitted, being too obviously a repetition of XXXVIII, 2 and 3, and having no natural significance in the mouth of Job.

THE TRAGEDY OF JOB

THE TRAGEDY OF JOB

Persons of the Drama

The Prologue
Job
Eliphaz the Temanite
Bildad the Shuhite
Zophar the Naamathite
Elihu the Buzite: a young man, leader of the Chorus —
The Chorus — a priestly group, with musical instruments,
Voice out of the Whirlwind
The Epilogue.

THE SCENE

The rise of the curtain reveals a village on the edge of the Arabian desert. It is twilight. In the foreground, slightly to the left, stands the house of Job, of white stone, a smooth, even surface broken with narrow black window slits; the sky is deep blue, streaked on the horizon with the yellow after-glow of the sunset; the shadows of the houses, trees, etc., on the ground are blue. The color of the vegetation has a blue tone. Toward the right almost on the edge of the scene stands an altar of unhewn stone. The village of white and yellow straggles away in the distance.[1]

The Prologue rises from before the altar and passes to the center of the stage.

[1] The scene was designed for the performance of the Harvard Menorah Society by Mr. Raymond Johnson of the Chicago Little Theatre Company.

Prologue

There was a man in the land of Uz, whose name was Job; and that man was perfect and upright, and one that feared God, and turned away from evil. And there were born unto him seven sons and three daughters. His substance was also seven thousand sheep, and three thousand camels, and five hundred yoke of oxen, and five hundred she-asses, and a very great household; so that this man was the greatest of all the children of the east. And his sons went and held a feast in the house of each one upon his day; and they sent and called for their three sisters to feast and to drink with them. And it was so, when the days of their feasting were gone about, that Job sent and sanctified them, and rose up early in the morning, and offered burnt offerings according to the number of all of them: for Job said, it may be that my sons have sinned and renounced God in their hearts. Thus did Job continually.

Now it came to pass on the day when the sons of God came to present themselves before Jehovah, that Satan also came among them. And Jehovah said unto Satan. Whence comest thou? Then Satan answered Jehovah, and said, " From going to and fro in the earth, and from walking up and down in it." And Jehovah said unto Satan, " Hast thou considered my servant Job? for there is none like him in the earth, a perfect and upright man, one that feareth God, and turneth away from evil." Then Satan answered Jehovah, and said, " Does Job fear God for nought? Hast not thou made a hedge about him, and about his house, and about all that he hath, on every side? thou hast blessed the work of his hands, and his substance is increased in the land. But put forth thy hand now, and touch all that he hath and he will renounce thee to thy face! " And Jehovah said unto Satan, " Behold, all that he hath is in thy power; only upon himself put not forth thy hand." So Satan went forth from the presence of Jehovah.

And it fell on a day when his sons and his daughters were eating and drinking wine in their eldest brother's house, that there came a messenger unto Job, and said, " The oxen were plowing, and the asses feeding beside them; and the Sabæans fell upon them, and took them away: yea; they have slain the servants with the edge of the sword; and I only am escaped alone to tell thee." While he was yet speaking, there came also another, and said: " The fire of God is fallen from heaven; and hath burned up the sheep and the servants, and consumed them; and I only am escaped to tell thee." While he was yet speaking there came also another, and said " The Chaldeans made three bands, and fell upon the camels, and have taken them away, yea, and slain the servants with the edge of the sword; and I only am escaped to tell thee." While he was yet speaking there came also another, and said: " Thy sons and thy daughters were eating and drinking wine in their eldest brother's house; and, behold, there came a great wind from the wilderness, and smote the four corners of the house, and it fell upon the young men and they are dead; and I only am escaped alone to tell thee.

Then Job arose, and rent his robe, and shaved his head, and fell down upon the ground, and worshipped; and he said, " Naked came I out of my mother's womb, and naked shall I return thither; Jehovah gave and Jehovah hath taken away; blessed be the name of Jehovah! " In all this Job sinned not, nor charged God foolishly.

Again it came to pass on the day when the sons of God came to present themselves before Jehovah, that Satan came also among them to present himself also before Jehovah. And Jehovah said unto Satan, " From whence comest thou? " And Satan answered Jehovah, and said,

" From going to and fro in the earth, and from walking up and down in it." And Jehovah said unto Satan, " Hast thou considered my servant Job? for there is none like him in the earth, a perfect and upright man, one that feareth God, and turneth away from evil: and he still holdeth fast his integrity, although thou movedest me against him, to destroy him without cause." And Satan answered Jehovah, and said, " Skin for skin, yea, all that a man hath will he give for his life. But put forth thy hand now, and touch his bone and his flesh, and he will renounce thee before thy face." And Jehovah said unto Satan, " Behold, he is in thy hands; only spare his life."

So Satan went forth from the presence of Jehovah, and smote Job with sore boils from the sole of his foot unto his crown. And he took him a potsherd to scrape himself therewith; and he sat among the ashes. Then said his wife unto him, " Dost thou still hold fast thine integrity? Renounce God, and die! " But he said unto her, " Thou speakest as one of the foolish women speaketh. What? shall we receive good at the hand of God, and shall we not receive evil? " In all this did not Job sin with his lips.

Now when Job's three friends heard of all this evil which was come upon him, they came every one from his own place: Eliphaz the Temanite, and Bildad the Shuhite, and Zophar the Naamathite; and they made an appointment together to come to bemoan him and to comfort him. And when they lifted up their eyes afar off, and knew him not, they lifted up their voices, and wept; and they rent everyone his robe, and sprinkled dust upon their heads toward heaven.

As he speaks the scene quietly grows darker. Just as he is about to finish lightning flashes across the stage, followed by a clap of thunder, and complete darkness. The darkness slowly dissipates into clear blue light, in which can be seen the ruins of Job's house. Against the sole upstanding beam stands Job, in rags, leaning on a stick.

As the morning advances, groups of the chorus, in twos and threes, stop round about him, pointing him out to each other and making comments in dumb show. When Eliphaz, Bildad, and Zophar have begun their discourse with Job, the chorus gathers round to listen.

Of the three friends, Bildad and Eliphaz enter together from the right. They make obeisance before the altar, and then stop before Job. Zophar follows with the same business a few seconds later. Then Job speaks.

Job

Let the day perish wherein I was born;
And the night which said, There is a man child conceived!
Let that day be darkness;
Let not God seek for it from above,
Neither let the light shine upon it!   5
Let darkness and the shadow of death claim it for their own;
Let all that maketh black the day terrify it!
As for that night, let thick darkness seize upon it;
Let it not rejoice among the days of the year;
Let it not come in to the number of the months!   10
Lo, let that night be barren;
Let no joyful voice come therein!
Let them curse it that curse the day,
Who are ready to rouse up leviathan!
Let the stars of the twilight thereof be dark!   15
Let it look for light, but have none;
Neither let it behold the eyelids of the morning:
Because it shut not up the doors of my mother's womb,
Nor hid trouble from mine eyes!
Why died I not from the womb?   20
Why did I not give up the ghost when my mother bare me?
Why did the knees receive me?

Or why the breasts, that I should suck?
For now should I have lien down and been quiet;
I should have slept; then had I been at rest,   25
With kings and counsellors of the earth,
Who built up waste places;
Or with princes that had gold,
Who filled their houses with silver;
Or as an hidden untimely birth I had not been;   80
As infants who never saw light,
— In nothingness.

There the wicked cease from troubling;
And there the weary be at rest.
There the prisoners are at ease together;   85
They hear not the voice of the taskmaster.
The small and the great are there;
And the servant is free from his master.

Wherefore is light given to him that is in misery,
And life unto the bitter in soul?   40
Who long for death, but it cometh not;
And dig for it more than for hidden treasures;
Who rejoice exceedingly
And are glad when they can find the grave.
Why is light given to a man whose way is hid,   45
And whom God hath hedged in?

For my sighing cometh before I eat,
And my groanings are poured out like water.
For the thing which I fear cometh upon me,
And that which I am afraid of cometh unto me.   50
I am not at ease, neither am I quiet,
Neither have I rest: but trouble cometh!

Dawn has been breaking during the speech and now the

*clear sharp light of the morning fills the scene. The
Chorus, led by Elihu, marches across the stage, from the
village to the altar, chanting:*

Shemà Yisrael, Yahweh Elohenu, Yahweh Ehad!
The Lord giveth and the Lord taketh away
Blessed be the name of the Lord.   55

*Elihu burns on the altar incense which flashes up in a
straight, instantaneous yellow flame and subsides. During the ceremony, the crowd, Eliphaz, Bildad, and Zophar
worship, facing the altar. Job alone stands in his original
position, unmoved, and apparently immovable. When the
ceremony is over, the Chorus marches back to centre stage,
and the three friends turn to Job.*

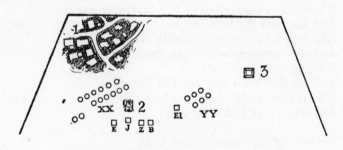

1. The Village
2. The Ruin of Job's House
3. The Altar

xx — Chorus
yy — Chorus
J. Job
E. Eliphaz

Z. Zophar
B. Bildad
El. Elihu

Eliphaz

If one assay to commune with thee, wilt thou be grieved? —
But who can withhold himself from speaking?
Behold, thou hast instructed many,
And thou hast strengthened the weak hands.
Thy words have upholden him that was falling,   65
And thou hast made firm the feeble knees.
But now it is come unto thee, and thou faintest,
It toucheth thee, and thou art troubled.
Is not thy fear of God thy confidence,
And the integrity of thy ways thy hope?   70
Remember, I pray thee, who ever perished, being innocent?
Or where were the upright cut off?
According as I have seen, they that plow iniquity,
And sow trouble, reap the same.
By the breath of God they perish,   75
And by the blasting of his anger are they consumed.
The roaring of the lion, and the voice of the fierce lion,
And the teeth of the young lions are broken.
The old lion perisheth for lack of prey,
And the whelps of the lioness are scattered abroad.   80

Now a thing was secretly brought to me,
And mine ear receiveth a whisper thereof.
In thoughts from the visions of the night,
When deep sleep falleth on men,
Fear came upon me and trembling,   85
Which made all my bones to shake.
Then a spirit passed before my face;
The hair of my flesh stood up.
It stood still, but I could not discern the appearance thereof;
A form was before mine eyes: 90
There was silence, and I heard a voice, saying
" Shall mortal man be more just than God?

Shall a man be more pure than his Maker?
Behold, he putteth no trust in his servants;
And his angels he chargeth with folly: 95
How much more them that dwell in houses of clay,
Whose foundation is in the dust,
Who are crushed before the moth!
Betwixt morning and evening they are destroyed: 100
They perish for ever without any regarding it.
Is not their tent-cord plucked up within them?
They die, and that without wisdom."

Call now: is there any that will answer thee?
And to which of the holy ones wilt thou turn?   105
For vexation killeth the foolish man,
And jealousy slayeth the silly one.
I have seen the foolish taking root:
But suddenly God cursed his habitation.
His children are far from safety,   110
And they are crushed in the gate,
Neither is there any to deliver them,
Whose harvest the hungry eateth up,
And taketh it even out of the thorns,
And the snare gapeth for their substance.   115
For affliction cometh not forth from the dust,
Neither doth trouble spring out of the ground;
But a man is born unto trouble,
As sparks fly upward.

But as for me, I would seek God,   120
And unto God would I commit my cause:
Who doeth great things and unsearchable,
Marvelous things without number:
Who giveth rain upon the earth,
And sendeth waters upon the fields: 125
So that he setteth up on high those that be low,

And those who mourn are exalted to safety;
He frustrateth the devices of the crafty,
So that their hands cannot perform their enterprise.
He taketh the wise in their own craftiness; 130
And the counsel of the cunning is carried headlong.
They meet with darkness in the day-time,
And grope at noonday as in the night.
But he saveth from the sword of their mouth,
Even the needy from the hand of the mighty. 135
So the poor hath hope,
And Iniquity stoppeth her mouth.

(*very solemnly*)

Behold, happy is the man whom God correcteth:
Therefore despise not thou the chastening of the Almighty.
For he maketh sore, and he bindeth up; 140
He woundeth, and his hands make whole.
He will deliver thee in six troubles,
Yea, in seven there shall no evil touch thee.
In famine he will redeem thee from death;
And in war from the power of the sword. 145
Thou shalt be hid from the scourge of the tongue;
Neither shalt thou be afraid of destruction when it cometh.
At destruction and dearth thou shalt laugh:
Neither shalt thou be afraid of the beasts of the earth.
For thou shalt be in league with the stones of the field; 150
And the beasts of the field shall be at peace with thee.
And thou shalt know that thy tent is in peace;
And thou shalt visit thy fold and shalt miss nothing.
Thou shalt know also that thy seed shall be great,
And thine offspring as the grass of the earth. 155
Thou shalt come to thy grave in a full age,
Like as a shock of grain in its season.
Lo this, we have searched it, so it is;
Hear it, and know it for thy good.

Job

Oh that my vexation were but weighed,   160
And all my calamity laid in the balances!
For now it would be heavier than the sand of the seas!
Therefore have my words been rash.
For the arrows of the Almighty are within me,
The poison whereof my spirit drinketh up: 165
The terrors of God do set themselves in array against me.
Doth the wild ass bray when he hath grass?
Or loweth the ox over his fodder?
Can that which hath no savour be eaten without salt?   170
Or is there any taste in the white of an egg? —
Things that my soul refused to touch,
Lo! they are as my loathsome food.
Oh, that I might have my request,
And that God would grant me the thing that I long for! 175
Even that it would please God to crush me;
That he would let loose his hand and cut me off!
Then should I yet have comfort;
For what is my strength that I should wait?
And what is mine end, that I should be patient?   180
Is my strength the strength of stone?
Or is my flesh of brass?
Is it not that I have no hope in me,
And that prosperity is driven quite from me?
(placing his hand on Eliphaz's shoulder)
To him that is ready to faint kindness should be showed
      from his friend;   185
Even to him that forsaketh the fear of the Almighty.
(Bildad and Zophar turn away)
My brethren have dealt deceitfully as a brook,
As the channel of brooks that pass away,
Which are black by reason of the ice,
And wherein the snow hideth itself;   190

What time they wax warm, they vanish;
When it is hot, they are consumed out of their place.
(*They turn back*)
The caravans that travel by the way of them turn aside,
They go up into the waste and perish.
The caravans of Tema looked,   195
The companies of Sheba waited for them;
They were put to shame because they had hoped;
They came thither and were confounded.

For ye are like thereto.
Ye see a terror, and are afraid.   200
Did I say, Give unto me?
Or, Offer a present for me of your substance?
Or, Deliver me from the adversary's hand?
Or, Redeem me from the hand of oppressors?
And, Cause me to understand wherein I have erred?   205
How forcible are words of uprightness,
But your reproof, what doth it reprove!
Do ye imagine to reprove words?
Seeing that the speeches of one that is desperate are as
    wind.
Yea, ye would cast lots upon the fatherless,   210
And make merchandise of your friend. (*They turn away,
    with deprecating gestures*)
Now therefore be pleased to look upon me;
For surely I shall not lie to your face.
Return, I pray you, let there be no injustice;
Yea, return again, my cause is righteous.   215
Is there any injustice on my tongue?
Cannot my palate discern wrong things? (*They face him
    again, reluctantly. Job proceeds with biting incisive-
    ness.*)
Is there not a warfare to man upon earth?
And are not his days like the days of an hireling?

As a servant that earnestly desireth the shadow,   220
And as an hireling that looketh for his wages?
So am I made to possess months of misery,
And wearisome nights are appointed to me.
When I lie down, I say, When shall I arise
And the night be gone?   225
And I am full of tossings to and fro
Unto the dawning of the day.
My flesh is clothed with worms and clods of dust;
My skin healeth and breaketh out afresh.
My days are swifter than a weaver's shuttle,   230
And are spent without hope.
Oh, remember that my life is a breath,
Mine eye shall no more see good.
The eye of him that seeth me shall behold me no more.
(*To Eliphaz*)
Thine eyes shall be upon me, but I shall not be.   235
As the cloud is consumed and vanisheth away,
So he that goeth down to Sheol shall come up no more.
He shall return no more to his house,
Neither shall his place know him any more.
Therefore I will not refrain my mouth; (*as Eliphaz offers
    to silence him*)   240
I will speak in the anguish of my spirit;
I will complain in the bitterness of my soul. (*Turning
    toward the altar.*)

Am I a sea, or a sea-monster,
That thou settest a watch over me?
When I say, My bed shall comfort me,   245
My couch shall ease my complaint:
Then thou scarest me with dreams,
And terrifiest me through visions:
So that my soul chooseth strangling
And death rather than these my bones.   250

I loathe my life;
I would not live alway;
Let me alone,
For my days are vanity.
For what is man, that thou shouldest magnify him,   255
And that thou shouldest set thy mind upon him,
And that thou shouldest visit him every morning,
And try him every moment?
How long wilt thou not look away from me,
Nor let me alone till I swallow down my spittle?   260
If I have sinned, what do I unto thee, O thou watcher of
      men?
Why hast thou set me as a mark for thee,
So that I am a burden to myself?
And why dost thou not pardon my transgression,
And take away mine iniquity?   265
For now shall I lie down in the dust;
And thou wilt seek me diligently, but I shall not be!

Bildad

How long wilt thou speak these things?
And how long shall the words of thy mouth be like a mighty
      wind?
Doth God pervert justice?   270
Or doth the Almighty pervert righteousness
If thy children have sinned against him,
And he have delivered them into the hand of their transgres-
      sion?
If thou wouldest seek diligently unto God
And make thy supplication to the Almighty;   275
If thou wert pure and upright, surely now he would awake
      for thee,
And make the habitation of thy righteousness prosper.
And though thy beginning was small,

Yet thy latter end would greatly increase.
For inquire, I pray thee, of the former age, 280
And apply thyself to that which the fathers have searched
out:
(For *we* are but of yesterday, and know nothing,
Because our days upon earth are a shadow:)
Shall not they teach thee and tell thee,
And utter words out of their heart? 285
Can papyrus grow without mire?
Can the Nile-grass grow without water?
Whilst it is yet in its greenness, and not cut down,
It withereth before any other herb.
So are the paths of all that forget God; 290
And the hope of the godless man shall perish:
His confidence shall break in sunder,
His trust is in a spider's web.
He shall lean upon his house, but it shall not stand:
He shall hold fast thereby, but it shall not endure. 295
He is green before the sun, and his shoots go forth over his
garden —
His roots — are wrapped about the stone-heap, he beholdeth
the place of stones!
If he be destroyed from his place,
Then it shall deny him, saying, I have not seen thee.
Lo! this is the end his life shall find, 300
And out of the earth shall others spring.
Behold: God will not cast away a perfect man,
Neither will he uphold the evil-doers.
He will yet fill thy mouth with laughter.
And thy lips with songs of gladness. 305
They that hate thee shall be clothed with shame,
And the tent of the wicked shall be no more.

Job

Of a truth I know that it is so:

But how can man be just with God?
If God be pleased to contend with him,   310
Man cannot answer him one in a thousand.
God is wise in heart and mighty in strength:
Who hath hardened himself against him and prospered?
Him who removeth mountains and they know it not,
When he overturneth them in his anger.   315
Who shaketh the earth out of its place,
And the pillars thereof tremble.
Who commandeth the sun and it riseth not,
And sealeth up the stars.
Who alone stretcheth out the heavens,   320
And treadeth upon the waves of the sea.
Who maketh the Bear, Orion, and Pleiades,
And the chambers of the south.
Who doeth great things past finding out;
Yea, marvellous things without number.   325

Lo, he goeth by me, and I see him not:
He glideth on, but I perceive him not:
Behold, he seizeth the prey, who can hinder him?
Who will say unto him, What doest thou?
God will not hold back his anger;   330
The helpers of Rahab do stoop under him.
How much less shall I answer him,
And choose out my words to reason with him!

For him, though I be righteous, would I have no answer;
Yet him, my judge, must I supplicate.   335
So, if I had called, and he had answered me;
Yet would I not believe that he hearkened unto my voice.
For he breaketh me with a tempest,
And multiplieth my wounds without cause.
He will not suffer me to take my breath,   340
But filleth me with bitterness.

If we speak of strength,
Lo, he is mighty!
And if of justice,
Who, saith he, will summon me?   345
Though I be righteous, mine own mouth shall condemn me:
Though I be perfect, it shall prove me perverse.
I am perfect,
I regard not myself;
I despise my life.   350
It is all one; therefore I say,
He destroyeth the perfect and the wicked.

If pestilence slay suddenly,
And the guiltless perish — he laughs.
The earth is given into the hand of the wicked: 355
He covereth the faces of the judges thereof.
If it be not he,
Who then is it?   (*The friends hide their faces at the
     blasphemy.*)
Now my days are swifter than a post:·
They flee away, they see no good.   360
They are passed away as swift ships;
As the eagle that swoopeth on the prey.
If I say,
"I will forget my complaint,
I will put off my sad countenance,   365
And be of good cheer,"
I am afraid of all my sorrows,
I know that he will not hold me innocent.
I shall be condemned:
Why then do I labour in vain?   370
If I wash myself with snow water,
And make my hands never so clean,
Yet will he plunge me in the ditch,
And mine own clothes shall abhor me.

For he is not a man as I am, that I should answer him,   375
That we should come together in judgment;
There is no umpire betwixt us,
That might lay his hand upon us both;
Let him take his rod away from me,
And let not his terror make me afraid,   380
Then would I speak and not fear him:
For I am no coward in myself.

My soul is weary of my life;
I will give free course to my complaint;
I will speak in the bitterness of my soul.   385
I will say unto God (*toward the altar again*) Do not condemn me;
Shew me wherefore thou contendest with me.
Is it good unto thee that thou shouldest oppress,
That thou shouldest despise the work of thine hands,
And shine upon the counsel of the wicked?   390
Hast thou eyes of flesh,
Or seest thou as man seeth?
Are thy days as the days of men,
Or thy years as man's days,
That thou inquirest after mine iniquity,   395
And searchest after my sin,
Although thou knowest that I am *not* wicked,
And there is none that can deliver out of thine hand?
Thine hands have framed me
And fashioned me together round about;   400
Yet thou dost destroy me.
Remember, I beseech thee, that thou hast fashioned me as clay;
And wilt thou bring me into dust again?
Hast thou not poured me out like milk,
And curdled me like cheese?   405
Thou hast clothed me with skin and flesh,

And knit me together with bones and sinews.
Thou hast granted me life and lovingkindness,
And thy visitation hath preserved my spirit.
Yet these things thou didst hide in thine heart;   410
I know that this is with thee:
If I sin, then thou markest me,
And thou wilt not acquit me from mine iniquity.
If I be wicked, woe is me; and if I be righteous, yet shall
    I not lift up my head,
Being filled with ignominy,   415
And looking upon my affliction.
And if my head exalt itself,
Thou huntest me as a lion,
And again thou showest thyself marvellous upon me.
Thou renewest thy witnesses against me,   420
And increasest thine indignation upon me;
Changes and warfare are with me.
Wherefore then hast thou brought me forth out of the womb?
I had given up the ghost, and no eye had seen me.
I should have been as though I had not been;   425
I should have been carried from the womb to the grave.
Are not my days few?
Cease then, and let me alone,
That I may take comfort a little
Before I go whence I shall not return —   430
Even to the land of darkness and of the shadow of death:
The land dark as midnight,
The land of the shadow of death, without any order;
And where the light is as midnight.

   *Zophar (indignant, with uplifted hand, to Bildad and
       Eliphaz trying to hold him back.)*
Should not the multitude of words be answered?   435
And should a man full of talk be justified?
(to Job)

Should thy boastings make men hold their peace?
And when thou mockest, shall no man make thee ashamed?
For thou sayest, My doctrine is pure,
And I am clean in mine own eyes.   440
But O that God would speak,
And open his lips against thee;
And that he would show thee the secrets of wisdom;
For he is manifold in understanding!

Know therefore that God exacteth of thee   445
Less than thine iniquity deserveth.

Canst thou by searching find out God!
Canst thou find out the Almighty unto perfection?
It is high as heaven;
What canst thou do?   450
Deeper than Sheol;
What canst thou know?
The measure thereof is longer than the earth,
And broader than the sea.
If he pass through, and imprison,   455
And bring unto judgment, then who can hinder him?
For he knoweth false men:
He seeth iniquity also, even though he consider it not.

But vain man is void of understanding,
Yea, man is born as a wild ass's colt.   460
(*pleadingly*)
If thou set thine heart aright,
And stretch out thine hands toward him;
If iniquity be in thine hand, put it far away,
And let not unrighteousness dwell in thy tents;
Surely then shalt thou lift up thy face without spot;   465
Yea, thou shalt be stedfast, and shalt not fear;

For thou shalt forget thy misery;
Thou shalt remember it as waters that are passed away:
And thy life shall be clearer than noonday;
Though there be darkness, it shall be as the morning.   470
And thou shalt be secure,
Because there is hope;
Yea, thou shalt search about thee,
And shalt take thy rest in safety.
Also thou shalt lie down,   475
And none shall make thee afraid;
Yea, many shall make suit unto thee.
But the eyes of the wicked shall fail,
And they shall have no way to flee,
And their hope shall be the giving up of the ghost.   480

Job

No doubt but ye are the people,
And wisdom shall die with you.
But I have understanding as well as you;
I am not inferior to you:
Yea, who knoweth not such things as these?   485
(*ironically*)
" Doth not the ear try words,
   " Even as the palate tasteth its meat?
" With aged men is wisdom,
   " And in length of days understanding."
I am as one that is the laughing-stock to his neighbor, 490
I who called upon God, and he answered,
The just, the perfect man is a laughing-stock.
In the thought of him that is at ease there is contempt for
      misfortune,
It is ready for them whose foot slippeth.
The tents of robbers prosper,   495
And they that provoke God are secure,
Into their hand God bringeth abundantly.

But ask now the beasts, and they shall teach thee;
And the fowls of the air, and they shall tell thee;
Or speak to the earth, and it shall teach thee: 500
Who knoweth not in all these that " the hand of the Lord
    hath wrought this? "
In whose hand is the soul of every living thing,
And the breath of all mankind.
(*reciting rapidly, almost as if by rote, to show that he is
    perfectly familiar with these things.*)
With him is wisdom and might:
He hath counsel and understanding.   505
Behold, he breaketh down,
And it cannot be built again;
He shutteth up a man,
And there can be no opening.
Behold, he withholdeth the waters,   510
And they dry up.
Again he sendeth them out,
And they overturn the earth.
With him is strength and sound wisdom;
The deceived and the deceiver are his.   515
He leadeth counsellors away spoiled,
And judges maketh he fools.
He looseth the bond of kings,
And bindeth their loins with a girdle.
He leadeth priests away stripped.   520
And overthroweth the mighty.
He removeth the speech of the trusty,
And taketh away the understanding of the elders.
He poureth contempt upon princes,
And looseth the belt of the strong.   525
He uncovereth deep things out of darkness,
And bringeth out to light the shadow of death.
He increaseth the nations,
And destroyeth them;

He enlargeth the nations, 530
And leadeth them captive.
He taketh away understanding from the chiefs of the people
of the earth,
And causeth them to wander in a wilderness where there is
no way.
They grope in the dark without light,
And he maketh them stagger like a drunken man. 535

Lo, mine eye hath seen all this,
Mine ear hath heard and understood it.
What ye know, the same do I know also:
I am not inferior unto you.
Surely I *would* speak to the Almighty, 540
And I *desire* to reason with God.
But ye are forgers of lies,
Ye are all physicians of no value.
Oh, that ye would altogether hold your peace,
And it should be your wisdom. 545
Hear now my reasoning,
And hearken to the pleadings of my lips.
Will ye speak unrighteously for God,
And talk deceitfully for his sake?
Will ye be partizans for him? 550
And special pleaders in his cause?
Is it good that he should search you out?
Or as one deceiveth a man, will ye deceive him?
He will surely reprove you,
If ye do secretly show favor to him. 555
Shall not his majesty make you afraid,
And his dread fall upon you?
Your memorable sayings are proverbs of ashes,
Your defences are defences of clay.
(*The chorus murmurs indignantly, Eliphaz tries to inter-
rupt.*)

Hold your peace, let me alone, that I may speak   560
And let come on me what will.
At all adventures I will take my flesh in my teeth,
And put my life in mine hand.
Behold, he will slay me;
I have no hope.   565
Nevertheless I will maintain my ways before him:
Even this shall be my security;
That a hypocrite would not come unto him.

Hear diligently my speech,
And let my declaration be in your ears.   570
Behold now, I have set my cause in order:
I know that I am righteous.   (*Challenging all his audience,
    then God.*)
Who is he that will *refute* me this?
For then would I hold my peace and give up the ghost.
(*advancing toward the altar*)
Only do not two things unto me,   575
Then will I not hide myself from thy face:
Withdraw thine hand far from me;
And let not thy terror make me afraid:
Then call thou, and I will answer;
Or let me speak, and answer thou me.   580

How many are mine iniquities and sins?
Make me to know my transgression and my sin.
Wherefore hidest thou thy face,
And holdest me for thine enemy?
Wilt thou harass a driven leaf?   585
And wilt thou pursue the dry stubble?
For thou writest bitter things against me,
And makest me to inherit the iniquities of my youth:
Thou puttest my feet also in the stocks,
And markest all my paths;   590

Thou drawest thee a line about the soles of my feet:
Though I am like a rotten thing that consumeth,
Like a garment that is moth-eaten.

Man that is born of a woman
Is few of days and full of trouble;   595
He cometh forth like a flower, and is cut down,
He fleeth also as a shadow and continueth not.
And dost thou open thine eyes upon such an one,
And bringest me into judgment with thee?
Who can bring a clean thing out of an unclean? Not
    one!   600
Seeing his days are determined,
The number of his months is with thee,
And thou hast appointed his bounds that he cannot pass;
Look away from him, that he may rest,
Till he shall accomplish, as an hireling, his day.   605
For there is hope of a tree, if it be cut down,
That it will sprout again,
And that the tender branch thereof will not cease;
Though the root thereof wax old in the earth,
And the stock thereof die in the ground,   610
Yet through the scent of water will it bud,
And put forth boughs like a plant.
But man dieth, and is laid low:
Yea, man giveth up the ghost, and where is he?
As waters fail from the sea,   615
And the river wasteth and drieth up,
So man lieth down and riseth not;
Till the heavens be no more he shall not awake,
Nor be roused out of his sleep.

Oh, that thou wouldest hide me in Sheol,   620
That thou wouldest keep me hidden, until thy wrath be
    spent,

That thou wouldest appoint me a set time and remember
    me!

— If a man die, shall he live again? —
(*musingly*)
Then all the days of my warfare would I wait, till my
    release should come;
Thou shouldest call, and I would answer thee: 625
Thou wouldest have a desire to the work of thine hands.—
(*with a gesture of despair*)
But now thou numberest my steps:
Dost thou not watch over my sin?
My transgression is sealed in a bag,
And thou fastenest up mine iniquity.   630
But as the mountain falling cometh to nought,
And the rock is removed out of its place,
The waters wear the stones,
The overflowings thereof wash away the dust of the earth,
So thou destroyest the hope of man: 635
Thou prevailest for ever against him, and he passeth;
Thou changest his countenance, and sendest him away;
His sons come to honour, and he knoweth it not;
And they are brought low, but he perceiveth it not of
    them;
But his flesh upon him hath pain,   640
And his soul within him mourneth.

Elihu (at the altar)

Where shall wisdom be found?
And where is the place of understanding?

Semichorus I

Surely there is a mine for silver
And a place for gold which they refine.   645

Iron is taken out of the earth,
And copper is molten out of the stone.
Man setteth an end to darkness
And seeketh out to the farthest bound
The stones from obscurity and thick darkness.　　650
He breaketh open a shaft away from where men sojourn
Where no foot passeth; hanging,
Swinging, to and fro,
Whilst the earth whence bread comes
Is turned up as by fire beneath.　　655
Its stones are places of sapphires
And it holds clods with gold.

A Member of the Chorus

But where shall wisdom be found?
And where is the place of understanding?

Semichorus II

That path no bird of prey knows　　660
Nor hath eye of falcon seen it;
The proud beasts have not trodden it,
Nor hath the fierce lion passed it.
Man putteth forth his hand upon the flinty rock;
He turneth the mountains by the roots.　　665
He cutteth out channels among the rocks;
He bindeth the streams that they trickle not;
And his eye seeth every precious thing.
And the thing that is hid bringeth he forth to light.

Elihu

But where shall wisdom be found?　　670
And where is the place of understanding?

Semichorus I

Man knoweth not the price thereof;

Neither is it found in the land of the living.
The deep saith, It is not in me:
And the sea saith, It is not with me.   675
It cannot be gotten for gold,
Neither shall silver be weighed for the price thereof.
It cannot be valued with the gold of Ophir,
Nor the precious onyx, nor the sapphire.
Gold and glass cannot equal it,   680
Neither shall it be exchanged for jewels of fine gold.
No mention shall be made of coral or of crystal:
Yea, the price of wisdom is above rubies.
The topaz of Ethiopia shall not equal it.
Neither shall it be valued with pure gold.   685

A Member of the Chorus

Whence then cometh wisdom
And where is the place of understanding?
It is hid from the eyes of all living,
And kept close from the fowls of the air!

Elihu

Destruction and Death say,   690
We have heard a rumor thereof with our ears.
God understandeth the way thereof,
And he knoweth the place thereof.
For he looketh to the ends of the earth,
And seeth under the whole heaven   695
To make a weight for the wind;
Yea, he meteth out the waters by measure.
When he made a decree for rain,
And a way for the lightning of thunder,
Then did he see it and declare it;   700
He established it, yea, and searched it out.
And unto man said,

Full Chorus

Behold, the *fear* of the Lord, that is wisdom:
And to depart from evil is understanding.

*The relative position of the players has now been shifted.
The Chorus is divided, half by the altar, the rest in the
centre, Job and his friends are at the extreme left. The
lighting is a warm orange, the strong yellow-orange of
tropical midday.*

Eliphaz

Should a wise man make answer with vanities,   705
And fill his belly with the east wind?
Should he reason with unprofitable talk,
Or with speeches wherewith he can do no good?
Yea, thou doest away with fear,
And hinderest devotion before God.   710
For thy speech teacheth thee,
And thou choosest the tongue of the crafty.
Thine own mouth condemneth thee, and not I;
Yea, thine own lips testify against thee.
Art thou the first man that was born?   715
Or wast thou brought forth before the hills?
Hast thou heard the secret counsel of God?
And dost thou limit wisdom to thyself?
What knowest *thou*, that *we* know not?
What understandest thou, which is not in us?   720
With us are both the grayheaded and the very aged men,
Much elder than thy father.
Are the consolations of God too small for thee,
Even the word that is gentle with thee?
Why doth thine heart carry thee away?   725
And why do thine eyes flash,
That thou turnest thy spirit against God,
And lettest such words go out of thy mouth?

What is man, that he should be clean?
And he who is born of a woman, that he should be right-
    eous? 730
Behold, God putteth no trust in his holy ones;
Yea, the heavens are not clean in his sight:
How much less one that is abominable and corrupt,
A man that drinketh iniquity like water!

I will show thee, hear thou me; 735
And that which I have seen I will declare:
(Which wise men have heard from their fathers, who have
    hid it;
They to whom alone the land was given.
Unto whom no stranger yet had come:)
The wicked man travaileth with pain all his days, 740
Even the number of years that are laid up for the op-
    pressor.
A sound of terrors is in his ears;
In prosperity the destroyer shall come upon him:
He believeth not that he shall return out of darkness,
And he is waited for of the sword: 745
He wandereth abroad for bread, saying, Where is it?
He knoweth that the day of darkness is ready at his hand:
Distress and anguish make him afraid;
They prevail against him, as a king ready to the battle
Because he hath stretched out his hand against God, 750
And behaveth himself proudly against the Almighty;
He runneth upon him with a stiff neck,
With the thick bosses of his bucklers;
Because he hath covered his face with his fatness,
And made collops of fat on his flanks: 755
And he hath dwelt in desolate cities,
In houses which no man inhabited,
Which were ready to become heaps.
He shall not be rich, neither shall his substance continue,

Neither shall his possessions be extended on the earth. 760
He shall not depart out of darkness;
The flame shall dry up his branches,
And by the breath of God's mouth shall he go away.
Let him not trust in vanity, deceiving himself:
For vanity shall be his recompense. 765
It shall be accomplished before his time,
And his branch shall not be green.
He shall shake off his unripe grape as the vine,
And shall cast off his flower as the olive tree.
For the company of the godless shall be barren, 770
And fire shall consume the tents of bribery.
They conceive mischief,
And bring forth iniquity,
And their heart prepareth deceit.

Job

I have heard many such things: 775
Miserable comforters are ye all.
Shall vain words have an end?
Or what provoketh thee that thou answerest?
I also could speak as ye do;
If your soul were in my soul's stead, 780
I could join words together against you,
And shake mine head at you.
But I would strengthen you with my mouth,
And the solace of my lips should assuage your grief.
Though I speak, my grief is not assuaged: 785
And though I forbear, what am I eased?
But now he hath made me weary:
(*Toward the altar*)
Thou hast made desolate all my company.
And thou hast laid fast hold on me, and the strength of
    thy grip is taken to be witness against me:

My very leanness riseth up against me, it testifieth to my
    face. 790
(*To his friends*)
He hath torn me in his wrath, and persecuted me;
He hath gnashed upon me with his teeth:
Mine adversary sharpeneth his eyes upon me.
They have gaped upon me with their mouth;
They have smitten me upon the cheek reproachfully: 795
They gather themselves together against me.
God delivereth me to the ungodly,
And casteth me into the hands of the wicked.
I was at ease, and he brake me asunder;
Yea, he hath taken me by the neck, and dashed me to
    pieces: 800
He hath also set me up for his mark.
His archers compass me round about,
He cleaveth my reins asunder, and doth not spare;
He poureth out my gall upon the ground.
He breaketh me with breach upon breach; 805
He runneth upon me like a giant.
I have sewed sackcloth upon my skin,
And have laid my horn in the dust.
My face is foul with weeping,
And on my eyelids is the shadow of death; 810
— Although there is no violence in mine hands,
And my prayer is pure.
(*He pauses a minute — the friends smile mockingly. He
            continues, enraged*)
O earth, cover not thou my blood,
And let my cry have no resting place!
My friends scoff at me 815
But even now, behold, my witness is in heaven,
(*The friends laugh quietly*)
And he that voucheth for me is on high.
Mine eye poureth out tears unto him,

That he should maintain the right of a man with God,
(*They laugh aloud*)
As a son of man pleadeth for his neighbor.   820
For when a few years are come,
I shall go the way whence I shall not return.
My spirit is consumed, my days are extinct,
The grave is ready for me.
Surely there are mockers with me,   825
And mine eye abideth in their provocation.
(*Toward the altar*)
Give now a pledge, be surety for me thyself;
Who else is there that will strike hands with me?
(*Sweeping the scene in appeal*)
For thou hast hid their heart from understanding:
Therefore shalt thou not exalt them.   830
(*To the friends*)
He that denounceth his friends for a prey,
Even the eyes of his children shall fail.
(*Zophar spits at him, while others grunt " Sinner! Liar!*
Enemy of God! ")
He hath made me also a byword of the people;
And they spit in my face.
Mine eye also is dim by reason of sorrow,   835
And all my members are as a shadow.
My days are past, my purposes are broken off,
Even the thoughts of my heart —
They change the day into night:
The light, say they, is near unto darkness.   840
My couch have I spread in the darkness.
I look for hope, Sheol is mine house;
I have said to corruption, Thou art my father;
To the worm, Thou art my mother, and my sister;
Where now is my hope?   845
And as for my welfare — who shall see it?
I shall go down to the bars of Sheol,

And rest forever in the dust —

> #### Bildad (*interrupting angrily*)
> How long will ye lay snares with words?
> Heed me, thou, and let me speak.   850
> Wherefore are we counted as beasts,
> And are become unclean in thy sight?
> Thou that tearest thyself in thine anger,
> Shall the earth be forsaken for thee?
> Or shall the rock be removed out of its place?   855
> (*The Chorus makes a menacing movement toward Job*)

> #### Job
> Oh, as for you all,— come on now again,
> For I find not a wise man among you:
> Upright men shall be astonied at this
> And the pure shall bestir themselves against the hypocrites
> Yea, the righteous man *shall* yet hold on his way: 860
> And he that is clean of hands shall wax stronger and
>   stronger!

> #### Bildad (*talking him down, taking the words out of his mouth*)
> Yea, the light of the wicked *shall* be put out,
> And the spark of his fire shall *not* shine.
> The light shall be dark in his tent,
> And his lamp above him shall be put out.   865
> The steps of his strength shall be straitened,
> And his own counsel shall cast him down.
> For he is cast into a net by his own feet,
> And he walketh upon the toils.
> A gin shall take him by the heel,   870
> And a snare shall lay hold on him.
> A noose is hid for him in the ground,

And a trap for him in the way.
Terrors shall make him afraid on every side,
And shall chase him at his heels.   875
His strength shall be hungerbitten,
And calamity shall be ready at his side.
It shall devour the members of his body,
Yea, the firstborn of death shall devour his members.
He shall be rooted out of his tent wherein he trusteth; 880
And he shall be brought to the king of terrors.
There shall dwell in his tent that which is none of his:
Brimstone shall be scattered upon his habitation.
His roots shall be dried up beneath,
And above shall his branch be cut off.   885
His remembrance shall perish from the earth,
And he shall be driven from light into darkness,
And chased out of the world.
He shall have neither son nor son's son among his people,
Nor any remaining where he sojourned.   890
They that come after shall be astonied at his day,
As they that went before were affrighted.
Surely such are the dwellings of the unrighteous,
And this is the place of him that knoweth not God.

Job

How long will ye vex my soul,   895
And break me in pieces with words?
These ten times have ye reproached me:
Ye are not ashamed that ye deal hardly with me.
And be it indeed that I have erred,
Mine error remaineth with myself.   900
If indeed ye *will* magnify yourselves against me,
And plead against me my reproach,
Know then that God hath wronged me in my cause,
And hath compassed me with his net.

Behold, I cry out " Violence ! "   905
But I am not heard;
I cry for help,
But there is no justice.
He hath walled up my way that I cannot pass,
And hath set darkness in my paths.   910
He hath stripped me of my glory,
And taken the crown from my head.
He hath broken me down on every side, and I am gone:
And mine hope hath he plucked up like a tree.
He hath also kindled his wrath against me,   915
And he counteth me unto him as one of his adversaries,
His troops come on together, and cast up their way against
    me,
And encamp round about my tent.
He hath put my brethren far from me,
And mine acquaintance are wholly estranged from me. 920
My kinsfolk have failed,
And my familiar friends have forgotten me.
They that dwell in mine house, and my maids, count me
    for a stranger;
I am an alien in their sight.
I call unto my servant, and he giveth me no answer,   925
Though I intreat him with my mouth.
My breath is strange to my wife,
And my supplication to the children of my own mother.
Even young children despise me;
If I arise, they speak against me.   930
All my inward friends abhor me,
And they whom I loved are turned against me.
My bone cleaveth to my skin and to my flesh,
And I am escaped with the skin of my teeth.
Have pity upon me, O ye my friends,   935
For the hand of God hath touched me!
Why do ye persecute me as God,

And are not satisfied with my flesh?
(*He pauses; peers at friends in appeal: they remain un-
moved. Then with a sudden burst*)
Oh that my words were now written! 940
Oh that they were inscribed in a book!
That with an iron pen and lead
They were graven in the rock for ever!
I know that my avenger liveth,
And that he shall stand up at the last upon the earth! 945
— My reins are consumed within me —
(*He falls to the ground. Zophar tries to help him up, but
Job shrinks away from him. Zophar shows he is offended*)
If ye say, How we will persecute him!
And that the root of the fault is found in me;
Be ye afraid of the sword:
For wrath bringeth the punishments of the sword, 950
That ye may know there is a judgment —

Zophar

(*interrupting, speaking across Job to Bildad*)
Therefore do my thoughts give answer to me,
Even by reason of my haste that is in me.
I have heard the reproof which putteth me to shame,
And the spirit of my understanding answereth me. 955
(*Turning to Job*)
Knowest thou not this of old time,
Since man was placed upon earth,
That the triumphing of the wicked is short,
And the joy of the godless but for a moment?
Though his height mount up to the heavens, 960
And his head unto the clouds;
Yet he shall perish for ever like his own dung:
They that have seen him shall say, Where is he?
He shall fly away as a dream, and shall not be found:
Yea, he shall be chased away as a vision of the night. 965

The eye which saw him shall see him no more;
Neither shall his place any more behold him.
His children shall seek the favour of the poor,
And his hands shall give back his own wealth.
His bones are full of his youth,   970
But it shall lie down with him in the dust.
Though wickedness be sweet in his mouth,
Though he hide it under his tongue;
Though he spare it, and will not let it go,
But keep it still within his mouth;   975
Yet his food in his bowels is turned,
It is gall of asps within him.
He hath swallowed down riches,
And shall vomit them up again:
God shall cast them out of his belly.   980
He shall suck the poison of asps:
The viper's tongue shall slay him.
He shall not look upon the rivers,
The flowing streams of honey and butter.
That which he laboured for shall he restore,   985
And shall not swallow it down;
According to the substance that he hath gotten,
He shall not rejoice.
For he hath oppressed and forsaken the poor;
He hath violently taken away a house and he shall not
    build it up.   990
Because he knew no quietness in his greed,
He shall not save aught of that wherein he delighteth.
There was nothing left that he devoured not,
Therefore his prosperity shall not endure.
(*Turning again to Bildad*)
In the fulness of his sufficiency   995
He shall be in straits:
The hand of every one that is in misery shall come upon
    him.

When he is about to fill his belly,
God will cast the fierceness of his wrath upon him,
And will rain it upon him while he is eating.   1000
He shall flee from the iron weapon,
And the bow of brass shall strike him through;
He draweth it forth and it cometh out of his body:
Yea, the glittering point cometh out of his gall;
Terrors are upon him;   1005
All darkness is laid up for his treasures:
A fire not blown by man shall devour him;
It shall consume that which is left in his tent.
The heavens shall reveal his iniquity,
And the earth shall rise up against him.   1010
The increase of his house shall depart,
His goods shall flow away in the day of his wrath
This is the portion of a wicked man from God.
And the heritage appointed unto him by God.

Job

Hear diligently my speech,   1015
And let this be your comfort unto me.
(*Bildad and Zophar try to interrupt*)
Suffer me, that I may also speak:
And after that I have spoken, mock on.
Gaze on me — is my complaint to man?
And why should I not be impatient?   1020
Look unto me, and be astonished,
And lay your hand upon your mouth.

For even the memory of this troubles me,
(*His eyes fixed, as if he were seeing a vision*)
— Wherefore do the wicked live,
Become old, yea, wax mighty in power?   1025
Their seed is established with them in their sight,
And their offspring before their eyes.

Their houses are safe from fear,
Neither is the rod of God upon them.
Their bull gendereth, and faileth not,   1030
Their cow calveth, and casteth not her calf.
They send forth their little ones like a flock,
And their children dance,
They sing to the timbrel and harp,
And rejoice at the sound of the pipe.   1035
They spend their days in prosperity,
And in a moment they go down to Sheol.
Yet they said unto God, " Depart from us,
For we desire not the knowledge of thy ways.
What is the Almighty that we should serve him?   1040
And what profit should we have if we pray unto him? "

Eliphaz (interrupting)

Lo, their prosperity is not in *their* hand:
The defense of the wicked is far from *me*.

Job

How oft is it that the lamp of the wicked is put out?
How oft cometh their calamity upon them?   1045
That God distributeth sorrows in his anger?
That they are as stubble before the wind,
And as chaff that the storm carrieth away?

Bildad (interrupting)

God layeth up their iniquity for their *children*.

Job

Let God recompense it unto the wicked himself, that him-
     self may know it!   1050
Let his own eyes see his destruction,
And let *him* drink of the wrath of the Almighty.

For what careth he for his house after him,
When the number of his months is cut off in the midst?

Zophar (interrupting)

Shall any teach God knowledge,   1055
Seeing he judgeth those that are high?

Job

(with a gesture of despair at his friends' stupidity)

One dieth in his full strength,
Being wholly at ease and quiet:
His pails are full of milk,
And the marrow of his bones is moistened.   1060
And another dieth in bitterness of soul,
And never tasteth of good.
They lie down alike in the dust,
And the worm covereth them.

> *Eliphaz*
>   God's —
> *Bildad*
>   Behold —   *(interrupting together)*
> *Zophar*
>   Wherefore —

Job (impatiently continuing)

Behold, I know your thoughts,   1065
And the devices wherewith ye would wrong me.
For ye say, " Where is the house of the prince?
And where is the tent wherein the wicked dwelt? "
Have ye not asked wayfaring men?
And do ye not know their evidences —   1070
That the evil man is spared in the day of calamity?
That he is led away from the day of wrath?

Who shall declare his way to his face?
And who shall requite him what he hath done?
He shall be borne to the grave;   1075
And men shall keep watch over his tomb.
The clods of the valley shall be sweet unto him,
And all men draw after him,
As there went innumerable before him.
How then comfort ye me in vain,   1080
Seeing in your answers there remaineth only falsehood.

(*Bildad, Zophar pass into the village in disgust. Job looks after them a moment, then passes to the side of the altar.*

Elihu, steps forward at the head of the Chorus, marching slowly toward the altar.)

Elihu (*chanting*)

1. There are that remove the land marks;
   They violently take away flocks and feed them.
   They drive away the ass of the fatherless —

2. They take the widow's ox for a pledge,   1085
   They turn the needy out of the way.
   The poor of the earth all hide themselves.

3. Behold, as wild asses in the desert the wicked go forth
        to their work,
   Seeking diligently for their food:
   The wilderness yieldeth them bread for their chil-
        dren.   1090

4. They cast their provender in the fields;
   And they glean the vintage of the wicked,
   They lie all night naked without clothing.

5. And have no covering in the cold,

They are wet with the showers of the mountains.　1095
And embrace the rock for want of shelter.

Full Chorus

1. The wicked pass swiftly away upon the face of the
     waters
   Their portion is cursed in the earth,
   Into the ways of the vineyards they turn not;

2. As drought and heat consume the snow waters,　1100
   So *Sheol* consumeth them who have sinned;
   The womb shall forget them,

3. The worm feed sweet on them;
   They shall be no more remembered.
   Yea, even as a tree, unrighteous shall broken be.　1105

A Man of the Chorus

1. There are that pluck the fatherless from the breast,
   And take a pledge of the poor:
   So that they go about naked without clothing.

2. And being hungry they carry sheaves,　1110
   They make all within the walls of those wicked men,
   They tread their wine presses and suffer thirst.

3. From out of the populous city men groan
   And the soul of the wounded crieth out.
   Yet God regardeth not the evil.　　　　1115

4. These are of them that rebel against the light,
   That they know not the ways thereof
   Nor abide in the paths thereof:

5. The murderer who riseth with the light,

He killeth the poor and the needy   1120
And in the night he is a thief.

6. The eye also of the adulterer waiteth for twilight:
Saying, No eye shall see me,
And he covers his face with a mask.

7. These, in the dark dig through houses,   1125
In the daytime they shut themselves up,
They know not the light.

8. For as the thick darkness
Is morning to all of them,
For the terror of thick darkness they know.   1130

Full Chorus

1. Yea, God preserveth these mighty ones by his power,
Even them that devour the unbearing barren,
And do no good to the widow.

2. They rise up when they believe not they should live,
God giveth them to be in security, and they rest
therein,   1135
But his eyes are upon their ways;

3. They are exalted; yet a little, and they are gone:
Yea, they are brought low, they are taken out of the
way as all others
And are cut off as the tops of the ears of the grain.

*The illumination is now the same as that of the opening
of the first act, except for the persistence of the orange red
tints on the edge of the horzion, particularly, in the line
of the altar.*

*The Chorus is seen on the left — Eliphaz enters, right.
He pauses before Job at the altar. Job seeing him, rises*

and moves center. Eliphaz follows, speaking as he goes.

Eliphaz

Can a man be profitable unto God?   1140
Surely he that is wise is profitable unto himself.
Is it any pleasure to the Almighty that thou art righteous?
Or is it gain to him that thou makest thy ways perfect?
Is it for thy *fear* of him that he reproveth thee,
That he entereth with thee into judgment?   1145

Is not thy wickedness great?
Neither is there any end to thine transgressions.
Indeed, thou *hast* taken pledges of thy brother for nought,
And stripped the naked of their clothing.
Thou hast not given water to the weary to drink,   1150
And thou hast withholden bread from the hungry.
Thou, the mighty man, didst own the land,
Didst in honour dwell therein.
But thou hast sent widows away, stripped,
And the arms of the fatherless have been broken.   1155
Therefore snares are round about thee,
And sudden fear troubleth thee,
Darkness that defies thine eye,
And abundance of waters cover thee.

Is not God in the height of heaven?   1160
And behold the stars above, how high they are!
Thou sayest therefore, "What doth God know?
Can he judge through the thick darkness?
Thick clouds are a covering to him, that he seeth not;
And he walketh in the vault of heaven."   1165
Wilt thou keep the old way
Which wicked men have trodden?
Who were snatched away before their time,
Whose foundation was poured out as a stream:

Who said unto God, "Depart from us;"   1170
And, "What can the Almighty do for us?"

Job (*interrupting*)

Yet he filled their houses with good things:
While far from me their wicked counsel is.

Eliphaz (*without heeding the interruption*)

The righteous see it, and are glad;
And the innocent laugh them to scorn: 1175
Saying, Surely they that did rise up against us are cut off
And the remnant of them fire hath consumed.
(*Going to Job*)
Acquaint now thyself with God and be at peace:
Thereby good shall come unto thee.
Receive, I pray thee, the law from his mouth,   1180
And lay up his words in thine heart.
If thou return to the Almighty,
Thou shalt be built up;
Put away unrighteousness far from thy tents,
And lay thou thy treasure in the dust,   1185
And the gold of Ophir among the stones of the brooks;
Let the Almighty be thy treasure,
And precious silver unto thee.
Then shalt thou delight thyself in the Almighty,
And shalt lift up thy face unto God.   1190
Thou shalt make thy prayer unto him,
And he will hear thee;
And thou shalt pay thy vows.
Thou shalt also decree a thing,
And it shall be established unto thee;   1195
And light shall shine upon thy ways.
When they cast thee down,
Thou shalt say, There is lifting up;

Yea, the humble person will God save.
He will deliver even him that is not innocent: 1200
Yea, he shall be delivered through the cleanness of thy
    hands.

Job

Even so, my complaint is bitter:
My stroke is heavier than my groaning.
Oh that I knew where I *might* find him,
That I *might* come even to his seat!   1205
I would set my cause in order before him,
And fill my mouth with arguments.
I would know the words which he would answer me,
And understand what he would say unto me.

Would he contend with me in the greatness of his
    power?   1210
Nay, but he would give heed unto me;
For an upright man would be reasoning with him;
And I should be delivered for ever from my judge.
Yet behold, I go forward,
But he is not there;   1215
And backward,
But I cannot perceive him:
On the left hand, where he doth work,
But I cannot behold him;
He hideth himself on the right hand,   1220
I cannot see him.
But he knoweth the way that *I* take;
When he hath tried me, I shall come forth as gold.
(*Enter Bildad and Zophar from the village left*)
My foot hath held fast to his steps;
His way have I kept, and turned not aside.   1225
I have *not* gone back from the commandment of his lips;

I *have* treasured up the words of his mouth more than my
    necessary food.
But he hath a mind to a thing,
And who can turn him?
And what his soul desireth,   1230
Even that he doeth.
For he performeth that which is appointed for me:
And many such things are with him.

Therefore am I terrified at his presence;
When I consider, I *am* afraid of him.   1235
For *God* hath made my heart faint.
And alone the *Almighty* hath terrified me;
For I am not dismayed before the darkness,
Nor because thick darkness covereth my face.

Hoi! Why is it, seeing times are not hidden from the Al-
    mighty,   1240
That they who know him see not his ways?

Bildad

Dominion and fear are with God;
He maketh peace in his high places.
Is there any number to his armies?
And upon whom doth not his light arise?   1245
How then can man be just with God?
Or how can he be clean that is born of woman?
Behold even the moon hath no brightness,
And the stars are not pure in his sight:
How much less man, that is a worm!   1250
And the son of man, which is a worm!
The Shades tremble
Beneath the waters, and the inhabitants thereof.
Sheol is naked before him,

And destruction hath no covering.   1255
He stretcheth out the north over empty space.
And hangeth the earth upon nothing.
He bindeth up the waters in his thick clouds;
And the cloud is not rent under them.
He closeth in the face of his throne,   1260
And spreadeth his cloud upon it.
He hath described a boundary upon the face of the waters,
Unto the confines of light and darkness.
The pillars of heaven tremble
And are astonished at his rebuke.   1265
He stirreth up the sea with his power,
And by his understanding he smiteth through Rahab.
By his spirit the heavens are beautified;
His hand hath pierced the swift serpent.

Lo, these are but the outskirts of his ways;   1270
And how small a whisper do we hear of him!
Then the *thunder* of his power who can understand?

Job

How hast thou helped him that is *without* power!
How hast thou saved the arm that hath *no* strength!
How hast thou counselled him that hath *no* wisdom,   1275
And plentifully declared sound knowledge!
To whom hast thou uttered words?
And whose spirit came forth from thee?
As God liveth (*very slowly and solemnly*)
Who hath taken away my right;   1280
And the Almighty,
Who hath made my soul bitter —
—(For my life is yet whole in me,
And the spirit of God is in my nostrils:) —
Surely my lips shall not speak unrighteousness,   1285
Neither shall my tongue utter deceit.

Far be it from me that I should give you right.
Till I die I will not put away mine integrity from me;
My righteousness I hold fast, and will not let it go:
My heart shall not reproach me, so long as I live.   1290

Zophar

Let mine enemy be as the wicked,
And let him that riseth up against me be as the un-
     righteous!
What is the hope of the godless, though he get him gain,
When God taketh away his soul?
Will God hear his cry,   1295
When trouble cometh upon him?
Will he delight himself in the Almighty,
And call upon God at all times?
I will teach you concerning the hand of God;
That which is with the Almighty will I not conceal.   1300
Behold, all ye yourselves have seen;
Why then are ye become altogether vain?

This is the portion of a wicked man with God,
And the heritage of oppressors, which they receive from
     the Almighty: —
If his children be multiplied, it is for the sword;   1305
And his offspring shall not be satisfied with bread.
Those that remain of him shall be buried in death,
And his widows shall make no lamentation.
Though he heap up silver as the dust,
And prepare raiment as the clay;   1310
He may prepare it, but the just shall put it on,
And the *innocent* shall divide the silver.
He buildeth his house as the moth,
And as a booth which the keeper maketh.
He lieth down rich, but he shall not be gathered to his
     fathers;   1315

He openeth his eyes, and he is not.
Terrors overtake him like waters;
A tempest stealeth him away in the night;
The east wind carrieth him away, and he departeth,
And it sweepeth him out of his place.   1320
For God shall hurl at him and not spare;
He would fain flee out of his hand.
Men shall clap their hands at him,
And shall hiss him out of his place.
And if it be not so now, who will prove me a liar   1325
And make my speech nothing worth!

Job

Oh that I were as in the months of old,
As in the days when God watched over me:
When his lamp shined upon my head,
And by his light I walked through darkness;   1330
As I was in the ripeness of my days,
When the friendship of God was upon my tent;
When the Almighty was yet with me,
And my children were about me;
When my steps were washed with butter,   1335
And the rock poured me out rivers of oil!

When I went forth unto the gate of the city,
When I prepared my seat in the street,
The young men saw me and hid themselves,
And the aged rose up and stood;   1340
The princes refrained from talking,
And laid their hands upon their mouths;
The voice of the nobles was hushed,
And their tongues cleaved to the roof of their mouths.
For when the ear heard me, then it blessed me;   1345
And when the eye saw me, it gave witness unto me:
Because I delivered the poor that cried,

The fatherless also, that had none to help him.
The blessing of him that was ready to perish came upon
    me:
I caused the widow's heart to sing for joy.   1350
I put on righteousness and it clothed me:
My justice was as a robe and a diadem.
I was eyes to the blind,
And feet was I to the lame.
I was a father to the needy,   1355
And the cause of him that I knew not I searched out.
And I brake the jaws of the unrighteous,
And plucked the prey out of his teeth.
Then I said, I shall die in my nest,
And I shall multiply my days as the sand: 1360
My root is spread out to the waters,
And the dew lieth all night upon my branch:
My glory is fresh in me,
And my bow is renewed in my hand.

Unto me men gave ear and waited,   1365
And kept silence for my counsel.
After my words they spake not again;
And my speech distilled upon them;
And they waited for me as for the rain;
And they opened their mouth wide as for the latter
    rain.   1370
I smiled on them when they had no confidence;
And the light of my countenance they cast not down.
I chose out their way, and sat as chief,
And dwelt as a king in the army, as one that comforteth
    the mourners.
But now they that are younger than I have me in deri-
    sion,   1375
Whose fathers I disdained to set with the dogs of my
    flock:

— Yea, the strength of their hands, whereto should it
    profit me,
Men in whom ripe age is perished?
They are gaunt with want and famine;
They gnaw the dry ground,   1380
In the gloom of wasteness and desolation.
They pluck salt-wort by the bushes;
And the roots of the broom are their meat.
They are driven forth from the midst of men;
They are cried after as after a thief.   1385
So that they dwell in frightful valleys,
In the holes of the earth and of the rocks.
Among the bushes they bray;
Under the nettles they are gathered together.
They are children of fools, yea, children of base men; 1390
They were scourged out of the land —
And now am *I* become *their* song,
Yea, I am a byword unto them.
They abhor me, they stand aloof from me,
And spare not to spit in my face.   1395
For God hath loosed his cord and afflicted me,
And they have cast off the bridle before me.
Upon my right hand rise the rabble; they thrust at my feet,
And they cast up against me their ways of destruction:
They mar my path, they set forward my calamity,   1400
— Even men that have no helper —
As through a wide breach they come:
In the midst of the ruin they roll themselves upon me.
Terrors are turned upon me,
They chase mine honour as the wind;   1405
And my welfare is passed as a cloud.
And now my soul is poured out within me;
Days of affliction have taken hold upon me.
In the night season my bones are pierced in me,
And the pains that gnaw me take no rest.   1410

By God's great force is my garment disfigured:
It bindeth me about as the collar of my coat.
He hath cast me into the mire,
And I am become like dust and ashes.
(*Moving forward to the altar*)
I cry unto thee, and thou dost not answer me: 1415
I stand up, and thou gazest at me.
Thou art turned to be cruel to me:
With the might of thy hand thou persecutest me.
Thou liftest me up to the wind, thou causest me to ride
    upon it;
And thou dissolvest me in the storm. 1420
For I know that thou wilt bring me to death,
And to the house appointed for all living.

Howbeit doth not one stretch out the hand in his fall?
Or in his calamity therefore cry for help?
Did not I weep for him that was in trouble? 1425
Was not my soul grieved for the needy?
Yet when I looked for good, then evil came:
And when I waited for light, there came darkness.
My heart is troubled and resteth not;
Days of affliction are come upon me. 1430
I go mourning without the sun:
I stand up in the assembly, and cry for help.
I am a brother to jackals,
And a companion to ostriches.
My skin is black, and falleth from me, 1435
And my bones are burned with heat.
Therefore is my harp turned to mourning,
And my pipe into the voice of them that weep.

(*It is now the time for evening prayer. The Chorus is
    grouped about the altar. Elihu intones.*)
Shemá Yisrael,

Yahweh elohenu, Yahweh ehad   1440

Semichorus I

He gives and he takes away

Semichorus II

Blessed be the name of Yahweh

Full Chorus

Blessed be the name of Yahweh.

(Through all this Job alone stands unmoved. The Chorus and friends observing this, show their disapproval in various ways. Some spit on him, others pass him with indrawn skirts. Cries of " Sinner in Israel," " Stiff-necked," " Pool of Iniquity " are heard.)

Job (turning on them suddenly)

What portion should I have of God from above,
And what heritage of the Almighty from on high?   1445
Is there not calamity to the unrighteous,
And disaster to the workers of iniquity?

Doth not he see my ways,
And number all my steps?

If I walked with falsehood,   1450
And my foot hath hasted in deceit;
Let me be weighed in an even balance,
That God may know mine integrity;

If I did despise the cause of my manservant,
Or of my maidservant, when they contended with me: 1455
What then shall I do when God riseth up?
And when he visiteth, what shall I answer him?

Did not he that made me in the womb make him?
And did not one fashion us in the womb?
(*To Zophar*)
If my step hath turned out of the way,
And mine heart walked after mine eyes, 1460
And if any spot hath cleaved to mine hands:
Then let me sow, and let another eat;
Yea, let the produce of my field be rooted out.

If my land cry out against me, 1465
And the furrows thereof weep together;
If I have eaten the fruits thereof without money,
Or have caused the owners thereof to lose their life:
Let thistles grow instead of wheat,
And cockle instead of barley! 1470

If mine heart have been enticed unto a woman,
And I have laid wait at my neighbor's door:
Then let my wife grind unto another,
And let others bow down upon her.

If I have withheld the poor from their desire, 1475
Or have caused the eyes of the widow to fail,
Or have eaten my morsel alone,
And the fatherless have not eaten thereof,
— Nay, from my youth he grew up with me as with a
father.
And her have I guided, from my mother's womb! — 1480

If I have seen any perish for want of clothing,
Or that the needy had no covering,
If his loins have not blessed me,
And if he hath not been warmed with the fleece of my
sheep;
If I have lifted up my hand against the fatherless, 1485

Because I saw my partizans in the gate,
Then let my shoulder fall from my shoulder blade
And mine arm be broken from the bone.

If I have made gold my hope
And have said to the fine gold, Thou art my confi-
    dence;   1490
If I have rejoiced because my wealth was great
And because my hand had gotten much;
If I have beheld the sun when it shinèd,
Or the moon walking in brightness
And my heart hath been secretly enticèd   1500
And my mouth hath kissed my hand,
This also were an iniquity to be punished by the judges
For I should have denied the God that is above.

If I have rejoiced at the destruction of him that hated me
Or lifted up myself when evil found him —   1505
— Yea, I have not suffered my mouth to sin
By asking his life with a curse! —
If the men of my tent said not,
Who can find one that hath not been filled with his meat?
If the sojourner did lodge in the street;   1510
And I opened not my doors to the traveller;
If, like Adam, I covered my transgressions,
By hiding mine iniquity in my bosom;
Because I feared the great multitude
And the contempt of families terrified me,   1515
So that I kept silence, and went not out of the door:
Then —(*he makes a gesture of resignation — then with
    sudden force*)
Oh that I had the indictment which mine adversary hath
    written!
Surely I would carry it upon my shoulder:
I would bind it unto me as a crown!

I would declare unto him the number of my steps;   1520
As a prince would I present it to him! —
— Oh that I had one to hear me!
Lo, here is my signature — let God reply!

(He surveys them, turning slowly. For a moment they stand silent. Then Eliphaz offers to speak. Job turns from him saying:)
The words of Job are ended!

Semichorus I

Behold, now, behemoth, which God made as well as
   thee;   1525
He eateth grass as an ox.
Lo now, his strength is in his loins,
And his force is in the muscles of his belly:
He moveth his tail like a cedar:
The sinews of his thighs are knit together.   1530
His bones are as tubes of brass;
His limbs are like bars of iron.
He is the chief of the ways of God:
He only that made him giveth him his sword.
Surely the mountains bring him forth food,   1535
Where all the beasts of the field do play.
He lieth under the lotus-trees,
In the covert of the reed, and the fen.
The lotus-trees cover him with their shade;
The willows of the brook compass him about.   1540
Behold, if a river overflow he trembleth not;
He is confident, though a Jordan swell even to his mouth.
Shall any take him when he is on the watch,
Or pierce through his nose with a snare?

Semichorus II

Canst thou draw out leviathan with fishhook?   1545

Or press down his tongue with a cord?
Canst thou put a rope into his nose?
Or pierce his jaw through with a hook?
Will he make many supplications unto thee?
Or will he speak soft words unto thee? 1550
Will he make a covenant with thee,
That thou shouldst take him for a servant forever?
Wilt thou play with him as with a bird?
Or wilt thou bind him for thy maidens?
Will the bands of fishermen make traffic of him? 1555
Will they part him among the merchants?
Canst thou fill his skin with barbed irons,
Or his head with fish spears?
Lay thy hand upon him;
Remember the battle, and do so no more. 1560
Behold the hope of him is in vain:
Will not one be cast down even at the sight of him?
None is so fierce that he dare stir him up.
Who can strip off his outer garment?
Who shall come within his jaws? 1565
Who can open the doors of his face?
Round about his teeth is terror.
His strong scales are his pride,
Shut up together as with a close seal.
One is so near to another, 1570
That no air can come between them.
They are joined one to another;
They stick together, so that they cannot be sundered.
His sneezings flash forth light,
And his eyes are like the eyelids of the morning. 1575
Out of his mouth go burning torches,
And sparks of fire leap forth.
Out of his nostrils a smoke goeth,
As of a boiling pot and burning rushes.
His breath kindleth coals, 1580

And a flame goeth forth from his mouth.
In his neck abideth strength,
And terror danceth before him.
The flakes of his flesh are joined together;
They are firm upon him; they cannot be moved.   1585
His heart is as firm as a stone;
Yea, firm as the nether millstone.
When he raiseth himself up, the mighty are afraid:
By reason of consternation they are beside themselves.
If one lay at him with the sword, it cannot avail;   1590
Nor the spear, nor the dart, nor the pointed shaft.
He counteth as straw, all these,
And brass as rotten wood.
The arrow cannot make him flee:
Sling-stones are turned with him into stubble.   1595
Clubs are counted as stubble;
He laugheth at the rushing of the javelin.
His under parts are like sharp potsherds:
He spreadeth as it were a threshing-wain upon the mire.
He maketh the deep to boil like a pot: 1600
He maketh the sea like a pot of ointment.
He maketh a path to shine after him,
One would think the deep to be hoary.
Upon earth there is not his like,
That is made without fear.   1605
He looks down on every thing that is high:
He is king over all the sons of pride.

Elihu (coming forward slowly from the altar)

I am young, and ye are old:
Wherefore I held back, and durst not show you mine opinion.
I said, Days should speak,   1610
And multitude of years should teach wisdom.
Behold, I waited for your words,

I listened for your reasons,
Whilst ye searched out what to say.
Yea, I attended unto you,   1615
And, behold, there was none that convinced Job,
Or that answered his words, among you.
(*To Chorus*)
They are amazed, they answer no more:
They have not a word to say.
And shall I wait because they speak not,   1620
Because they stand still, and answer no more?
I also will show mine opinion.
The spirit within me constraineth me;
Behold, my breast is as wine which hath no vent;
Like new wineskins it is ready to burst.   1625
I will speak that I may find relief;
I will open my lips and answer.
(*To Job*)
Howbeit, Job, I pray thee, hear my speech,
And hearken to all my words.
If thou canst, answer thou me: 1630
Set thy words in order before me, stand forth.
Behold, I am toward God even as thou art.
I also am formed out of clay:
Behold, *my* terror shall *not* make thee afraid,
Neither shall *my* pressure be heavy upon thee.   1635
Surely thou hast spoken in mine hearing,
And I have heard the voice of thy words, saying,
" I am clean, without transgression;
" I am innocent, neither is there iniquity in me;
" Behold, God findeth occasions against me,   1640
" He counteth me for his enemy;
" He putteth my feet in the stocks,
" He marketh all my paths."
Lo, I will answer thee: in this thou art not just;
For God is greater than man.   1645

Why dost thou strive against him
Because he giveth not account of any of his matters?
For God speaketh once,
Yea twice, though man regardeth it not.

— In a dream, in a vision of the night,   1650
When deep sleep falleth upon men,
In slumberings upon the bed;
Then he openeth the ears of men,
And sealeth their instruction,
That he may withdraw man from his purpose,   1655
And hide pride from man;
He keepeth back his soul from the pit,
And his life from perishing by the sword.

Man is chastened also with pain upon his bed,
And with continual strife in his bones: 1660
So that his life abhorreth bread,
And his soul dainty food.
His flesh is consumed away, that it cannot be seen;
And his bones that were not seen stick out.
Yea, his soul draweth near unto the pit,   1665
And his life to the destroyers.

If there be with him an angel,
An interpreter, one among a thousand,
To shew unto man what is right for him;
Then God is gracious unto him, and saith,   1670
"Deliver him from going down to the pit,
I have found a ransom."
His flesh shall be fresher than a child's;
He returneth to the days of his youth;
He prayeth unto God,   1675
And God is favorable unto him;
So that he seeth his face with joy:

And he restoreth unto the man his righteousness.
Then singeth he before men, and saith, " I have sinned,
And perverted that which was right, and it profited me
    not: 1680
God hath redeemed my soul from going into the pit,
And my life shall behold the light."

Lo, all these things doth God work,
Twice, yea thrice, with a man;
To bring back his soul from the pit,   1685
That he may be enlightened with the light of the living.
Mark well, O Job, hearken unto me:
(*Job offers to speak*)
Hold thy peace, and I will speak.
(*changing his mind*)
If thou hast anything to say, answer me:
Speak thou, for I desire to justify thee.   1690
(*Elihu waits, looking to Job: Job turns his back. Elihu
         turns to the three Friends*)
Hear my words, ye wise men,
And give ear unto me, ye that have knowledge.
Job hath said, " I am righteous,
And God hath taken away my right:
Notwithstanding my right I am accounted a liar;   1695
My wound is incurable, though I am without transgression.
It profiteth a man nothing
That he should delight himself with God."
Therefore hearken unto me,
Ye men of understanding: 1700
Far be it from God, that he should do wickedness;
And from the Almighty, that he should commit iniquity.
For the *work* of a man will he render unto him,
And cause every man to find according to his ways.
Yea, of a surety, God will not do wickedly,   1705
Neither will the Almighty pervert justice.

Who gave him a charge over the earth?
Or who hath disposed the whole world?
Should he set his heart upon himself,
Should he gather unto himself his spirit and his breath, 1710
All flesh shall perish together,
And man shall turn again unto dust.
If now thou hast understanding, hear this:
Hearken to the voice of my words.
Shall even one that hateth justice govern? 1715
And wilt thou condemn him that is righteous and mighty?
Is it fit to say to a king, Thou art vile,
Or to nobles, Ye are wicked?
How much less to him that respecteth not the persons of
    princes,
Nor regardeth the rich more than the poor. 1720
For they all are the work of his hands.
In a moment they die, even at midnight;
The people are shaken and pass away,
And the mighty are taken away without hand.
For his eyes are upon the ways of a man, 1725
And he seeth all his goings.
There is no darkness, nor thick gloom,
Where the workers of iniquity may hide themselves.
For he needeth not further to consider a man,
That he should go before God in judgment. 1730
He breaketh in pieces mighty men in ways past finding out,
And setteth others in their stead.
Therefore he taketh knowledge of their works;
And he overturneth them in the night, so that they are
    destroyed.
He striketh them as wicked men 1735
In the open sight of others;
Because they turn aside from following him,
And would not have regard to any of his ways,
So that they caused the cry of the poor to come unto him,

And he heard the cry of the afflicted. 1740
When he giveth quietness, who then can condemn?
And when he hideth his face, who can behold him?
Alike, whether it be done unto a nation, or unto a man;
It is done that the godless man reign not, that there be none
    to ensnare the people.
For when any hath said unto God, 1745
" I have borne chastisement, I will not offend any more.
That which I see not teach thou me:
If I have done iniquity, I will do it no more,"
(*to Job, who turns his back*)
Shall his recompense be as thou wilt, that thou refusest it?
It is thou must choose, and not I: 1750
Therefore speak what thou knowest.
Men of understanding will say unto me,
Yea, every wise man that heareth me:
Job speaketh without knowledge,
And his words are without wisdom. 1755
(*to the friends*)
Would that Job were tried unto the end,
Because of his answering like wicked men.
For he addeth rebellion unto his sin,
He clappeth his hands among us,
And multiplieth his words against God. 1760
(*He pauses for a moment in the attitude of prayer, then
    turns to Job again. Job moves away, but Elihu follows
    him.*)
Thinkest thou this to be thy right,
Or sayest thou, " My righteousness is more than God's,"
That thou askest, What advantage will it be unto thee?
And, " What profit shall I have more than if I had sinned? "
I will answer thee, 1765
And thy companions with thee.
Look unto the heavens and see:

And behold the skies, which are higher than thou.
If thou hast sinned, what effectest thou against God?
And if thy trangressions be multiplied, what doest thou
    unto him?   1770
If thou be righteous, what givest thou him,
Or what receiveth he of thine hand?
Thy wickedness may hurt a man as thou art:
And thy righteousness may profit a son of man.
By reason of the multitude of oppressions men cry out; 1775
They cry for help by reason of the arm of the mighty.
But none saith, "Where is God my Maker,
Who giveth songs in the night;
Who teacheth us more than the beasts of the earth,
And maketh us wiser than birds of heaven?"   1780
There they cry but none giveth answer,
Because of the pride of evil men.
Surely God will not hear an empty cry,
Neither will the Almighty regard it.
How much less when thou sayest thou beholdest him
    not: 1785
The cause is before him, therefore wait for him!
But now because he hath not visited in his anger,
Thou sayest, He doth greatly regard arrogance:
— Thus doth Job open his mouth in vanity;
He multiplieth words without knowledge.   1790
(*His auditors show signs of impatience*)
Suffer me a little, and I will shew ye,
For I have yet somewhat to say on God's behalf.
I will fetch my knowledge from afar,
And will ascribe righteousness to my Maker.

A man of the Chorus

Behold, God is mighty,   1795
And despiseth not any;
He is mighty in strength of understanding.

He preserveth not the life of the wicked:
But giveth to the afflicted their right.
He withdraweth not his eyes from the righteous;   1800
But with kings upon the throne
He setteth them forever,
And they are exalted:
And if they be bound in fetters,
And be taken in the cords of affliction;   1805
Then he sheweth them their work and their transgressions,
That they have behaved themselves proudly.
He openeth also their ear to instruction,
And commandeth that they return from iniquity.
If they hearken and serve him,   1810
They shall spend their days in prosperity,
And their years in pleasantness.
But if they hearken not,
They shall perish by the sword,
And they shall die without knowledge.   1815
But they that are godless in heart lay up anger:
They cry not for help when he bindeth them.
They die in youth,
And their life perisheth among the unclean.
He delivereth the afflicted by their affliction,   1820
And openeth their ear in oppression.

Elihu

Yea, God would lure thee out of distress
Into a broad place, where there is no straitness;
And that which is set on thy table would be full of fatness.
But thou art full of the judgment of the wicked: 1825
Judgment and justice take hold of thee.
Because there is wrath, beware lest thou be led away by
     thy sufficiency.
Neither let the greatness of the ransom turn thee aside.
Will thy cry avail, that thou be not in distress,

Or all the forces of *thy* strength? 1830
Desire not the night, when peoples are cut off in their
    place.
Take heed, regard not iniquity:
For this hast thou chosen rather than affliction.
(*The low rumble of distant thunder is heard. As Elihu's
    speech progresses it grows steadily darker until the
    light is purple, and at the altar, livid.*)
Behold, God doeth loftily in his power:
Who is a teacher like unto him? 1835
Who hath enjoined him his way?
Or who can say, Thou hast wrought unrighteousness?
Remember that thou magnify his work,
Whereof men have sung.
All men have looked thereon; 1840
Man beholdeth it afar off.

A man of the Chorus

Behold, God is great, and we know him not;
The number of his years is unsearchable.
For he draweth up the drops of water,
Which distil in rain from his vapour: 1845
Which the skies pour down
And drop upon man abundantly.
Yea, can any understand the spreadings of the clouds,
The thunderings of his pavilion?

Elihu

Behold, he spreadeth his light around him; 1850
And he covereth the bottom of the sea.
For by these he judgeth the peoples;
He giveth meat in abundance.
He covereth his hands with the lightning;
And giveth it a charge that it strike the mark. 1855
The noise thereof telleth concerning him,

(*The noise of frightened cattle is heard*)
The cattle also concerning the storm that cometh up.
(*A flash of lightning and a loud peal of thunder: the storm
steadily increases*)
Yea, at this my heart trembleth,
And is moved out of its place,
Hear, O hear, the noise of his voice,   1860
And the sound that goeth out of his mouth.
He sendeth it forth under the whole heaven,
And his lightning unto the ends of the earth.
After it a voice roareth;
He thundereth with the voice of his majesty: 1865
And he restraineth not the lightning when his voice is
  heard.
God thundereth marvellously with his voice;
Great things doeth he,
Which we cannot comprehend.
For he saith to the snow,   1870
Fall thou on the earth;
Likewise to the shower of rain,
And to the showers of his storm of rain.
He sealeth up the hand of every man;
That all men whom he hath made may know it.   1875
Then the beasts go into coverts,
And remain in their dens.
Out of the chamber of the south cometh the storm:
And cold out of the north.
By the breath of God ice is given: 1880
And the stretch of the waters is straitened.
Yea, he ladeth the thick cloud with moisture;
He spreadeth abroad the cloud of his lightning:
And it is turned round about by his guidance,
That they may do whatsoever he commandeth them 1885
Upon the face of the habitable world:
Whether it be for correction,

Or for his land,
Or for lovingkindness, that he cause it to come.

*(The storm has become a whirlwind; lightning flashes
across the stage and plays about the altar. Then the
scene grows completely dark. There is a lull.)*

Hearken unto this, O Job: 1890
Stand still, and consider the wondrous works of God.
Dost thou know how God layeth his charge upon them,
And causeth the lightning of his cloud to shine?
Dost thou know the balancings of the clouds,
The wondrous works of him who is perfect in knowl-
    edge? 1900
How thy garments are warm
When the earth is still by reason of the south wind:
'Canst thou with him spread out the sky,
Which is strong as a molten mirror?
Teach us what we shall say unto him; 1905
For we cannot order our speech by reason of this dark-
    ness.
Shall it be told him that I would speak,
Or should a man wish that he were swallowed up?

*(The sound of the whirlwind is heard again. A low
vivid light appears on the horizon increasing in intensity
as the speech progresses, in a series of flashes about the
altar.)*

And now men see not the light which is bright in the skies
But the wind passeth and cleareth them. 1910
Out of the north cometh golden splendour:
God hath upon him a terrible majesty.
Touching the Almighty, we cannot find him out;
(Turning toward the altar and intoning)
He is excellent in power;
And in justice and plenteous righteousness he will not
    afflict.
Men do therefore fear him: 1915

He regardeth not any that are wise of heart.

(*The roar of the whirlwind gives place to a voice, the flashing light about the altar becomes steady and supernaturally clear. At the first sound the whole stage prostrates itself, each man prone, with face upon the ground. Job alone stands erect in centre stage.*)

Voice out of the Whirlwind

(*still, small, very penetrating*)

Who is this that darkeneth counsel by words without knowledge?

Gird up now thy loins like a man;

For I will demand of thee, and declare thou unto me.

Where wast thou when I laid the foundations of the earth? 1920

— Declare if thou hast understanding —

Who determined the measures thereof, if thou knowest?

Or who stretched the line upon it?

Whereupon were the foundations thereof fastened?

Or who laid the cornerstone thereof, 1925

When the morning stars sang together,

And all the sons of God shouted for joy?

Or who shut up the sea with doors,

When it brake forth, as if it had issued out of the womb;

When I made the cloud the garment thereof, 1930

And thick darkness a swaddling band for it,

And marked out for it my bound,

And set bars and doors,

And said, " Hitherto shalt thou come, but no further;

And here shall thy proud waves be stayed? " 1935

Hast thou commanded the morning since thy days began,

And caused the dayspring to know its place;

That it might take hold of the ends of the earth,

And the wicked be shaken out of it?

It is changed as clay under the seal; 1940

And all things stand forth as a garment:
And from the wicked their light is withholden,
And the high arm is broken.
Hast thou entered into the springs of the sea?
Or hast thou walked in the recesses of the deep?   1945
Have the gates of death been revealed unto thee?
Or hast thou seen gates of the shadow of death?
Hast thou comprehended the earth in its breadth?
Declare if thou knowest it all.

Where is the way to the dwelling of light,   1950
And of darkness, where is the place thereof;
That thou shouldest take it to the bound thereof,
And that thou shouldest discern the paths of the house
    thereof?
Hast thou entered the treasuries of the snow,
Or hast thou seen the treasuries of the hail,   1955
Which I have reserved against the time of trouble,
Against the day of battle and war?
By what way is the light parted,
Or the east wind scattered upon the earth?
Who hath cleft a channel for the waterflood,   1960
Or a way for the lightning of the thunder;
To cause it to rain on a land where no man is,
On a wilderness, wherein there is no man;
To satisfy the waste and desolate ground,
And to cause the tender grass to spring forth?   1965
Hath the rain a father?
Or who hath begotten the drops of dew?
Out of whose womb came the ice?
And the hoary frost of heaven, who hath gendered it?
The waters hide themselves and become like stone,   1970
And the face of the deep is frozen.

Canst thou bind the cluster of the Pleiades,

Or loose the bands of Orion?
Canst thou lead forth the Mazzaroth in their season?
Or canst thou guide the Bear with her train?   1975
Knowest thou the ordinances of the heavens?
Canst thou establish the dominion thereof in the earth?
Canst thou lift up thy voice to the clouds,
That abundance of waters may cover thee?
Canst thou send forth lightnings, that they may go,   1980
And say unto thee, Here we are?

Who hath put wisdom in the inward parts?
Or who hath given understanding to the mind?
Who can number the clouds by wisdom?
Or who can pour out the bottles of heaven,   1985
When the dust runneth into a mass,
And the clouds cleave fast together?

Canst thou hunt the prey for the lioness?
Or satisfy the appetite of the young lions,
When they couch in their dens,   1990
And abide in the covert to lie in wait?
Who provideth for the raven his prey,
When his young ones cry unto God,
And wander for lack of food?

Knowest thou the time when the wild goats of the rock
        bring forth?   1995
Or canst thou mark when the hinds do calve?
Canst thou number the months that they fulfill?
Or knowest thou the time when they bring forth?
They bow themselves, they bring forth their young,
They cast out their pains.   2000
Their young ones become strong,
They grow up in the open field;
They go forth, and return not again.

Who hath sent out the wild ass free?
Or who hath loosed the bands of the swift ass,   2005
Whose home I have made the wilderness,
And the salt land his dwelling place?
He scorneth the tumult of the city,
Neither heareth he the shoutings of the driver.
The range of the mountain is his pasture,   2010
And he searcheth after every green thing.

Will the wild-ox be content to serve thee?
Or will he abide by thy crib?
Canst thou bind the wild-ox with his band in the furrow?
Or will he harrow the valleys after thee?   2015
Wilt thou trust him, because his strength is great?
Or wilt thou leave to him thy labour?
Wilt thou confide in him, that he will bring home thy seed,
And gather the corn of thy threshing-floor?

The wing of the ostrich waves proudly;   2020
But are they the pinions and plumage of love?
For she leaveth her eggs on the earth,
And warmeth them in the dust,
And forgetteth that the foot may crush them,
Or that the wild beast may trample them.   2025
She dealeth hardly with her young ones as if they were not
    hers
Though her labour be in vain, she is without fear;
Because God hath deprived her of wisdom,
Neither hath he imparted to her understanding.
What time she lifteth up herself on high,   2030
She scorneth the horse and his rider.

Hast thou given the horse his might?
Hast thou clothed his neck with the quivering mane?
Hast thou made him to leap as a locust?

The glory of his snorting is terrible.   2035
He paweth in the valley, and rejoiceth in his strength:
He goeth out to meet the armed men.
He mocketh at fear and is not dismayed;
Neither turneth he back from the sword.
The quiver rattleth against him,   2040
The flashing spear and the javelin.
He swalloweth the ground with fierceness and rage:
Neither believeth he that it is the voice of the trumpet.
As oft as the trumpet soundeth he saith, Aha!
And he smelleth the battle afar off,   2045
The thunder of the captains, and the shouting.

Is it by thy wisdom, that the hawk soareth,
And stretcheth her wings toward the south?
Is it that the eagle mounteth up at thy command,
And maketh her nest on high?   2050
She dwelleth on the cliff, and maketh her home
Upon the point of the cliff and the stronghold.
From thence she spieth out the prey;
Her eyes behold it afar off.
Her young ones also suck up blood: 2055
And where the slain are there is she.

Shall he that cavilleth contend with the Almighty?
He that argueth with God, let him answer it.
(*The Voice gives way to the inarticulate storm, which fades
away in an instant.*)

Job.

I know thou canst do all things
And that no purpose of thine can be restrained.   2060

*The Voice out of the Whirlwind (beginning as a storm-noise
and growing into still articulateness).*
Who then is he that can stand before me?

Who hath first given unto me that I should repay him?
Whatsoever is under the whole heaven is mine.

Gird up thy loins now like a man:
I *will* demand of thee, and declare thou unto me.   2065
Wilt thou even annul my judgment?
Wilt thou condemn me, that thou mayest be justified?
Or hast thou an arm like God?
And canst thou thunder with a voice like him?
Deck thyself now with excellency and dignity;   2070
And array thyself with honor and majesty.
Pour forth the overflowings of thine anger:
And look upon everyone that is proud, and abase him.
Look on everyone that is proud, and bring him low;
And tread down the wicked where they stand.   2075
Hide them in the dust together;
Bind their faces in the hidden place.
Then also I will confess of thee
That thine own right hand can save thee.

Job

Behold, I am of small account; what can I
    answer thee?   2080
I lay mine hand upon my mouth.
Once have I spoken,— I will not speak again;
Yea twice; I will proceed no further.
I have spoken, but without understanding,
Things too wonderful, which I did not know.   2085
Only by hearsay had I known thee,
But now mine eye seeth thee,
And I recant my challenge and am comforted,
Amid dust and ashes.

The light at the altar becomes a vivid flash across the stage, and goes out leaving the scene dark for an instant.

Then slowly the lighting changes to blue and silver — a bright moonlight. The moon is clear, center stage.

The Chorus arises slowly and with signs of fear and awe move, left, into the village, out of sight.

Eliphaz, Zophar, and Bildad stand facing Job a moment, then with bent heads file out, right.

In the distance, from the village, is heard the faint intonation of the Chorus.

> Hear O Israel   2090
> Yahweh is our God, Yahweh alone
> He gives and he takes away
> Blest be the name of Yahweh forever.

Throughout this action Job stands immovable, his arms pressed over his breast, his head erect, in the full moonlight. The curtain falls and rises on an empty stage.

After a pause the EPILOGUE *comes forward.*

Epilogue.

And it was so, that after Yahweh had spoken these words unto Job, the Lord said to Eliphaz the Temanite, "My wrath is kindled against thee, and against thy two friends: for ye have not spoken of me the thing that is right, as my servant Job hath. Now, therefore, take unto you seven bullocks and seven rams, and go to my servant Job, and offer up for yourselves a burnt offering; and my servant Job shall pray for you; for him will I accept, that I deal not with you after your folly; for ye have not spoken of me the thing that is right, as my servant Job hath."

So Eliphaz the Temanite, and Bildad the Shuhite and Zophar the Naamathite went, and did according as Jehovah commanded them: and Yahweh accepted Job.

And Yahweh turned the captivity of Job, when he prayed for his friends: and Yahweh gave Job twice as much as he had before. Then came there unto him all his brethren, and all his sisters, and all they that had been of his acquaintance before, and did eat bread with him in his house: and they bemoaned him, and comforted him concerning all the evil that Yahweh had brought upon him: every man also gave him a piece of money, and every one a ring of gold.

So Yahweh blessed the latter end of Job more than his beginning: and he had fourteen thousand sheep, and six thousand camels, and a thousand yoke of oxen, and a thousand she-asses. He had also seven sons and three daughters. And he called the name of the first Jemimah; the name of the second, Keziah; and the name of the third, Keren-happuch. And in all the land were no women found so fair as the daughters of Job: and their father gave them inheritance among their brethren.

And after this Job lived an hundred and forty years, and saw his sons, and his son's sons, even four generations. So Job died, being old and full of days.

DRAMABOOKS

Hill and Wang has established DRAMABOOKS as a permanent library of the great classics of the theatre of all countries, in an attractive, low-priced format.

PLAYS

MD 1   *Christopher Marlowe* edited by Havelock Ellis. Introduction by John Addington Symonds
(Tamburlaine the Great, Parts I & II, Doctor Faustus, The Jew of Malta, Edward the Second)

MD 2   *William Congreve* edited by Alexander Charles Ewald. Introduction by Macaulay (Complete Plays)

MD 3   *Webster and Tourneur* Introduction by John Addington Symonds
(The White Devil, The Duchess of Malfi, The Atheist's Tragedy, The Revenger's Tragedy)

MD 4   *John Ford* edited by Havelock Ellis
(The Lover's Melancholy, 'Tis Pity She's a Whore, The Broken Heart, Love's Sacrifice, Perkin Warbeck)

MD 5   *Richard Brinsley Sheridan* edited with an Introduction by Louis Kronenberger
(The Rivals, St. Patrick's Day, The Duenna, A Trip to Scarborough, The School for Scandal, The Critic)

MD 6   *Camille and Other Plays* edited, with an Introduction to the well-made play by Stephen S. Stanton
(Scribe: A Peculiar Position, and The Glass of Water; Sardou: A Scrap of Paper; Dumas, *fils*: Camille; Augier: Olympe's Marriage)

MD 7   *John Dryden* edited, and with an Introduction by George Saintsbury
(The Conquest of Granada, Parts I & II, Marriage à la Mode, Aureng-Zebe)

MD 8   *Ben Jonson* edited, with an Introduction and Notes, by Brinsley Nicholson and C. H. Herford
(Volpone, Epicoene, The Alchemist)

MD 9   *Oliver Goldsmith* edited by George Pierce Baker with an Introduction by Austin Dobson
(The Good Natur'd Man, She Stoops to Conquer, An Essay on the Theatre, A Register of Scotch Marriages)

MD 10 *Jean Anouilh:* Selected Plays
(Antigone, Eurydice, The Rehearsal, Romeo and Jeannette, The Ermine)

MD 11 *Let's Get a Divorce! and Other Plays,* edited, and with an Introduction on The Psychology of Farce by Eric Bentley
(Labiche: A Trip Abroad, and Célimare; Sardou: Let's Get a Divorce!; Courteline, These Cornfields; Feydeau: Keep an Eye on Amélie; Prévert: A United Family; Achard: essay on Feydeau)

PLAYS (*continued*)

MD 12 *Jean Giraudoux* adapted and with an Introduction by Maurice Valency
(Ondine, The Enchanted, The Madwoman of Chaillot, The Apollo of Bellac

MD 13 *Jean Anouilh* Volume 2
(Restless Heart, Time Remembered, Ardèle, Mademoiselle Colombe, The Lark)

MD 14 *Henrik Ibsen: The Last Plays* Introduction and translation by William Archer
(Little Eyolf, John Gabriel Borkman, When We Dead Awaken)

MD 15 *Ivan Turgenev* translated by Constance Garnett
(A Month in the Country, A Provincial Lady, A Poor Gentleman)

MD 16 *George Farquhar* edited, with an Introduction and Notes, by William Archer
(The Constant Couple, The Twin-Rivals, The Recruiting Officer, The Beaux' Stratagem)

CRITICISM

D1 *Shakespeare and the Elizabethans* by Henri Fluchère. Foreword by T. S. Eliot
D2 *On Dramatic Method* by Harley Granville-Barker
D3 *George Bernard Shaw* by G. K. Chesterton
D4 *The Paradox of Acting* by Denis Diderot and *Masks or Faces?* by William Archer. Introduction by Lee Strasberg
D5 *The Scenic Art* by Henry James. Edited with an Introduction and Notes by Allan Wade
D6 *Preface to Hamlet* by Harley Granville-Barker
D7 *Hazlitt on Theatre* edited by William Archer and Robert Lowe. Introduction by William Archer
D8 *The Fervent Years* by Harold Clurman
D9 *The Quintessence of Ibsenism* by Bernard Shaw
D10 *Papers on Playmaking* edited by Brander Matthews
D11 *Papers on Acting* edited by Brander Matthews
D12 *The Theatre* by Stark Young
D13 *Immortal Shadows* by Stark Young
D14 *Shakespeare: A Survey* by E. K. Chambers
D15 *The English Dramatic Critics* edited by James Agate
D16 *Japanese Theatre* by Faubion Bowers
D17 *Shaw's Dramatic Criticism* (1895-98) edited by John F. Matthews
D18 *Shaw on Theatre* edited by E. J. West
D19 *The Book of Job as a Greek Tragedy* by Horace Meyer Kallen.